DIVORCE RECOVERY

🙡🙡🙡🙡🙡🙡🙡🙡🙡🙡🙡🙡🙡🙡🙡🙡

Healing the Hurt Through Self-Help and Professional Support

By
Allan J. Adler, M.D., and
Christine Archambault

This book is not intended to replace professional treatment or psychiatric counselling; there is no substitute for the experience and information that your doctor or mental health professional can provide. Rather, it is our hope that this book will provide additional information to help people understand the nature of divorce and the emotional and psychiatric disorders that can evolve.

Proper treatment should always be tailored to the individual. If you read something in this book that seems to conflict with your doctor or mental health professional's instructions, contact him/her. There may be sound reasons for recommending treatment that may differ from the information presented in this book.

If you have any questions about any of the information in this book, please consult your doctor or mental health care professional.

In addition, the names and cases used in this book do not represent actual people, but are composite cases drawn from several sources.

THE FACTS ABOUT ALVARADO PARKWAY INSTITUTE (API)

1-800-766-4API

PROGRAMS AT API INCLUDE:

INPATIENT SERVICES
- Chemical Dependency Treatment Services
  - Medical Detoxification
  - Rehabilitation Program
  - Renaissance Program
- Women's Program
  - Codependency
  - Sexual Abuse
  - Eating Disorders
  - Postpartum Depression
  - Divorce Recovery
- Depression Treatment Program
- Mental Health Services
  - Intensive Care Unit
  - Open Mental Health Program
- Adolescent and Childrens Services
  - Chemical Dependency
  - Mental Health
  - Dual Diagnosis
  - Complete Educational Services

OUTPATIENT SERVICES
- Chemical Dependency Outpatient Programs
  - Day Program
  - Evening Program
  - Dual Diagnosis
- Day Treatment Center
  - Adult Rehabilitation Program
  - Senior Program
  - Transitions Program
- Eating Disorders
- Weekend Family Program
  - Codependency Program
  - Divorce Recovery Program
  - Sexual Abuse Program
- Adolescent Chemical Dependency
- Adolescent Eating Disorders
- Child and Adolescent Partial Hospitalization Program

Alvarado Parkway Institute (API) is a private specialty hospital established to provide quality inpatient and outpatient care to children, adolescents, adults and families experiencing acute or chronic psychiatric illnesses or the incapacitating effects of addictive diseases. Our clinical philosophy emphasizes confidential, comprehensive individualized treatment within the context of a safe, caring and therapeutic environment.

API is staffed by a skilled team of professionials. Our treatment team includes psychiatrists, certified counselors, physicians, family therapists, occupational therapists, recreational therapists, art therapists, nutritionists and medical consultants. All members of the treatment team are involved in the therapeutic process from admission to discharge.

API is fully accredited by the Joint Commission on the Accreditation of Health Care Organizations and licensed by the California Department of Health. API is also a member of the National Association of Private Psychiatric Hospitals.

API is owned and operated by Psychiatric Institutes of America, a division of National Medical Enterprises.

Dedication

To my family, especially Allison and Michael, who were there in my time of need to supply the initial fuel for traveling the long road to my divorce recovery.

—Allan J. Adler, MD—

To Tasha Schaal, the other co-founder of Divorce Anonymous. Thank you for your creativity, enthusiasm and never ending emotional support. We need more like you on this planet!

—Christine Archambault—

Finally, we both dedicate this book to the readers who are struggling with the complex and painful issue of ending a relationship. It's difficult to even begin to explain the pain to another, much less believe they'd understand. We do. This book is about courage. Please don't be overwhelmed by what is in front of you. Reach inside yourself and find the strength to get the help you need. Work through the pain. The only way out is through.

Acknowledgments

Thanks to Richard Eamer for contributing the foreword. He had the original idea for this book and caused its creation because of his love for those special and innocent victims of divorce—the children.

We would like to thank Norm Zober and Bill Vickers of Psychiatric Institutes of America (PIA) for their support of this undertaking and for their continued presence in this endeavor.

We wish to thank Sharon McClure, MD, who was extremely helpful in this project.

We are grateful to the people at PIA Press, especially Dan Montopoli, Marilyn Devroye, Janet Chilnick and Larry Chilnick.

Our thanks also to Mae Rudolph, who's editorial assistance was essential in preparing the manuscript.

Dr. Adler wishes to acknowledge his patients, who have helped him grow, and the staff of Alvarado Parkway Institute, who rarely receive the recognition they deserve.... Thanks to Dr. Colarusso, whose patience, wisdom and constancy have stopped me from straying off course.... To my group, where I have learned that men feel, cry and laugh in their own special way.... Lastly, deepest gratitude to Susan Horrall, who is the best assistant in the universe....

Ms. Archambault wishes to express special thanks to those who went the extra mile to help in the early days of Divorce Anonymous: Terrie, Judie, Bhimi, Corky, Mary, Gwen, Hillary, Jan, Marlene, Rosa, Mort, and the Los Angeles NCJW.... Also thanks to my parents, Leonard and Susan McCullon, for the love and valuable lessons of childhood.

And lastly, we both want to express special thanks to those forever anonymous individuals who shared their pain and their breakthroughs in our groups. Without realizing it, they are true pioneers to whom we wish life's very best. They deserve it!

Contents

ALLAN J. ADLER, M.D.

DR. ALLAN J. ADLER is a graduate of Queens University, Kingston, Ontario, Canada, and is Board Certified in Psychiatry by the American Board of Psychiatry and Neurology.

He is the Medical Director of Alvarado Parkway Institute, (API), a 100 bed psychiatric hospital in San Diego and the Clinical Director of the Chemical Dependency Unit at API.

Dr. Adler is a past President of the San Diego Society of Psychiatric Physicians, a Fellow of the American Psychiatric Association, and is certified in alcoholism and other drug dependencies by the American Society of Addiction Medicine.

Dr. Adler has appeared extensively as an expert on emotional issues on television, radio and in public forums. He is in private practice in the San Diego area.

CHRISTINE ARCHAMBAULT

CHRISTINE ARCHAMBAULT (pronounced Ar-SHOM-bo) is co-founder and director of Divorce Anonymous. These are support groups for those undergoing divorce or separation.

Ms. Archambault is also involved in developing and implementing a Divorce Recovery program that will be offered in various hospitals across the country later next year. She has given workshops and facilitates support groups for individuals going through divorce.

Archambault, 41, attended State University of New York at Buffalo and is a member of the National Speakers Association.

FOREWORD

𝕽𝕽𝕽𝕽𝕽𝕽𝕽𝕽𝕽𝕽𝕽𝕽𝕽𝕽𝕽𝕽

BY RICHARD K. EAMER
CHAIRMAN AND
CHIEF EXECUTIVE OFFICER
NATIONAL MEDICAL ENTERPRISES

Divorce. It isn't a pretty word, and it isn't an enjoyable step to take. Let's face facts, though: divorce has become one of the hallmarks of modern American society. Half of all marriages in this country end in divorce. And when divorced people who have children remarry, there's only a *40 percent* chance that the marriage will survive.

Refusing to accept these realities doesn't make them go away. It just allows them to take us by surprise.

Divorce Recovery is not a pro-divorce book. Rather, it's a "be prepared" book. It's written especially for men and women whose marriages are already dissolving, and who want to face the inevitable with as much poise, maturity, and dignity as possible. I have seen too many friends and colleagues struggle with the emotional and financial burdens of divorce without knowing where and when to seek help. *Divorce Recovery* will give them the guidance they need.

As Chairman and Chief Executive Officer of National Medical Enterprises I have known and worked with both Allan Adler and Christine Archambault for many years. For over 15 years, Dr. Adler has served as medical director of Alvarado Parkway Institute, one of the finest hospitals in the National Medical Enterprises' Specialty Hospital Group. Ms. Archambault has recently been employed by NME to help establish Divorce Recovery programs throughout the chain of NME hospitals. Her previous work as the director and co-founder of *Divorce Anonymous* has served as excellent training for her new position.

Furthermore, each of the co-authors knows personally just how difficult separating from a loved one can be. Both of them are acutely aware of the shock, pain, anxiety, bitterness, and grief that threaten to overwhelm people who go through divorce. Neither of them would dream of advising divorce as soon as a couple starts to feel the strains of marital discord. They strongly advise people in a troubled relationship to seek individual counseling, couples counseling, or family counseling before they even begin to consider divorce as an option.

But Dr. Adler and Ms. Archambault are realists. They're well aware that divorce isn't always a mutual choice—and that even when it is, neither partner can fully anticipate all the disruptions it will cause.

■ They know that almost every divorce pits the "initiator," the one who suggests or demands divorce, against the "non-initiator," the one who didn't ask for and doesn't necessarily want divorce.

■ They know that when the pending divorce is announced, relatives and friends will have their say. Some will make hurtful remarks, accusing one or the other divorcing partner of failure. Others will simply grow silent, unthinkingly withdrawing support at a time when it's most needed.

■ They know that the presence of children vastly complicates both the practical and the emotional sides of divorce. Parents who divorce are still parents. Children of divorced parents still need and want both a mother and a father in their lives.

■ They know that people on the rebound after divorce often make unwise decisions. Some jeopardize their physical and emotional health in a frenzy of shallow sexual encounters. Others leap into an intimate relationship long before they're ready. Still others close themselves into a shell, growing depressed and despondent.

■ They know that people who remarry hope their own children and the new spouse (and possibly the new spouse's children from a former marriage, too) will immediately form a warm, close family unit—but they also know that instant stepfamily bliss is the exception, not the rule.

These are some of the gut-wrenching issues that surface in this book. *Divorce Recovery* doesn't advocate divorce. Rather, it takes the social reality of divorce as its starting point. Its admirable purpose is to give divorcing people realistic, no-nonsense, inside advice about surviving divorce and moving on.

Dr. Adler's and Ms. Archambault's straight talk, psychological probing, and self-help suggestions are bound to strike a responsive chord in anyone living through the emotional trauma of a marital breakup. Their detailed guide through the inner workings of divorce gently prepares the reader for the rough weeks and months that lie ahead, smoothing the way, illuminating the dark corners, and providing reassurance that survival and renewal are possible.

I wish divorce on no one. But to men and women who are already launched on that rough voyage, I commend *Divorce Recovery*, confident that its insights and practical suggestions will provide a beacon of light and hope. If you are living through the strain of divorce, I hope your life may be enriched by the reading of this timely and all too necessary book.

Richard K. Eamer
September, 1990

1

𒀭𒀭𒀭𒀭𒀭𒀭𒀭𒀭𒀭𒀭𒀭𒀭𒀭𒀭𒀭

THE EMOTIONAL COSTS
OF DIVORCE

*"Well, being divorced is like being hit by a Mack truck. If you
live through it, you start looking very carefully to the right and
to the left."*

—Jean Kerr, American playwright

*"Single life isn't always a picnic, but it's better than a bad
marriage."*

—Anon

The divorce isn't over when the papers are signed.

Most people think that once the legal hassle is over, the
suffering will be over and life will be normal again. This is not
the case. Divorce is not simply an episode, a distinct "happening" with a definite beginning and end. It is, instead, a transition, a process that begins long before the first visit to the
attorney and ends long after the moving van has driven away.

Most people who are thinking about divorce, are going
through a divorce, or have just gone through one hear a lot of
things about it—many of them as untrue as the belief that
divorce is simply a legal transaction.

You hear, for example, that divorce is a disaster, a nightmare.
You may also hear, in direct contradiction, that it's the beginning of an entirely happy new life, a chance to start fresh with
no burdens, no regrets, nothing but happiness and hope.

The truth is that your life may be better or it may be worse
(at least in the beginning). The only thing that is certain is that
it will be *different*. Whether it's better or worse will depend
almost entirely on how well you understand what's happening,

1

STAY TOGETHER OR SPLIT UP?

Of course, not all unhappy relationships end in divorce. Some improve with changing circumstances and the passage of time. Others improve in response to good, effective marriage counseling. Still others simply remain dysfunctional; nothing changes because neither spouse has the motivation to seek therapy or to ask for a divorce. In one out of every two American marriages, however, the time comes when at least one of the partners wants out. For whatever reasons, the divorce rate in the United States—50 percent—is the highest in the world.

---

how capable you are of insight, growth and change, and how much work you are willing to do to achieve recovery.

In dealing with divorce, you'll need as much awareness, effort, and help as with any other emotional catastrophe or crippling problem, such as alcoholism or drug addiction. In fact, in ways that will be seen, recovery from addictive illness can provide some important lessons for recovery from divorce.

Recovery can be an extraordinary opportunity for renewal and growth, and for building a life that's even better than the one before the divorce. Many people who have worked through the process of recovery from divorce (or other disabling emotional conditions, such as loss or addiction) actually say they're grateful for the experience. Despite the pain, or even because of it, such people have discovered a new self and a new way of living that is richer in understanding, unselfishness, and self-esteem because of the efforts they made during recovery.

However great the future may be, the "new beginning" or the "fresh start" does not and cannot begin until the recovery process begins. Whether the divorce is hostile or "friendly," whether you started it or the other partner did, divorce is a disjunction, a severance, a shock. It's a massive change, and for at least one partner, it is usually an unwelcome and unwanted change. Most people don't like change, anyway, and negative changes are especially unsettling and painful. Divorce means changes with powerful emotional consequences. If these are not to be permanently destructive—if they are to be turned into progress toward a better life—they require a period and a program of recovery.

WHY "RECOVERY"?

"Recovery" is a word carefully chosen to suggest that divorce resembles loss, illness, or an addictive disorder. To most people, divorce is like a death in the family; it's no accident that the stages of divorce have been compared to the stages of mourning. Divorce is surely among the three most traumatic things that can happen to a person; the death of a child is probably first, the death of a spouse the next.

Emotions that are common to divorcing people, and that should be expected and dealt with in recovery, include:

- loss and grief
- depression
- guilt
- anger
- self-hatred
- reduction in self-esteem
- fear
- anxiety
- regret
- isolation and loneliness

The loss is pervasive. A divorced person loses a family, a history, a past, a future, and perhaps most of all, an identity. In our society, a man and woman who get married are no longer merely two people who happen to live together with the blessing of the law or the church. They have become a couple: he is "husband" and she is "wife." Their legal, financial, and social lives will be shaped and, to an enormous degree, determined by their "coupling."

All sorts of matters become joint arrangements or decisions: where to live, how to spend money, what job to take, how to raise the children, whom to invite to dinner, where to go on vacation. On a deeper emotional level, people tend to change as they become part of a couple; they adjust or grow in tandem with each other, learn new habits, give up old ones, adopt some of the personality traits of the other person, or to some degree alter their own personality traits "to fit." This is particularly true of the more traditional coupling in which the wife becomes, to a small or great extent, secondary or even subservient to her husband. It has been said that two older people who have been married for a great many years begin to look alike. This is not so much because their physical features actually change, but because they begin to reflect each other's facial expressions and body language.

More than in any other human relationship, people find validation (or negation) of themselves in marriage. Good feelings about oneself are confirmed in the affection and approval of the partner; faults and shortcomings become more noticeable. People come to depend on their partners for advice, confirmation of their feelings and decisions, and relief from fears and pain. The tendency is to rely less upon one's own inner resources and more upon the partner's. When the partner disappears, many people may suddenly look in the mirror and ask, "Who am I, really?"

"Social identity" is also powerfully defined by marriage. People acquire an extended family and a circle of friends through marriage; you are no longer Mary and John but "my daughter and her husband," or "the Smiths," or "our neighbors the Smiths." The disruption of this status is most traumatic during the divorce process itself, just when support from family and close friends is so greatly needed.

Sadly, in our society, it seems to be generally accepted by divorced people (and everybody else) that divorce is something you "handle." You make the arrangements, deal with the lawyers and accountants and real estate agents, and then get on with your life. Divorce court itself is extremely impersonal. On the day your divorce is final, you go before the judge and sign a paper. The judge asks, "Is there anything else?" You say, "No," and that's it. It takes about two minutes. The next thing you know, you're in the elevator with a few strangers, going down to the parking lot, divorced and on your way home. There's no civilized ritual, no "funeral." There's no debriefing, no counseling. No one brings a casserole. Nothing. Later, some papers will arrive in the mail. That's all.

People sometimes say, "It takes two years to get over a divorce," but they assume you'll get over it by instinct and your own sheer force of character. Rarely do people tell you anything about how that "getting over" takes place. The supposition is that time takes care of it, as it does a bad cold. Aspirin, bed rest, and plenty of fluids will ease the symptoms, but you have to let nature take its course. What's perhaps even worse is the assumption that divorce, unlike death, serious illness, or other devastating episodes in life, is something people can handle on their own. Unlike these other problems, divorce is often seen as a "practical" matter— something that requires the aid of lawyers and accountants, but not psychological support or spiritual guidance.

Perhaps you can do it alone, as most people *appear* to. But speaking from personal experience, it's our conviction that asking for and getting help are vital parts of the recovery process, as they are in recovery from other emotional shocks. From our perspective, every divorce is really a double breakup. One half is the "legal divorce"—the actual proceedings by which you and your spouse separate your lives and your property. The other half is the "emotional divorce"—the vital, but most invisible, work of grieving for the past, coming to terms with the present, and planning for the future.

Recovery will be more rapid and more positive with help. It may even be that *only* with help can people reach that much-talked about "new life" and "new beginning."

THERAPY FOR DIVORCE

Although we are now approaching the twenty-first century, many of our ideas about divorce therapy are still plodding through the eighteenth or nineteenth. Despite the enormous growth of psychotherapy and self-help or group-support activities, especially in America, people still take a Victorian attitude toward divorce: You got yourself into this, you can get yourself out. Asking for help is admitting failure. Asking for help is sissy. Some people feel so much guilt over a broken marriage that they don't ask for help because they don't think they deserve it.

We believe, on the contrary, that asking for help is not a sign of weakness but of strength. It's a statement that you want to be a strong and responsible person, get back to normal as a functioning, contributing human being, and (if you're a parent) be in the best possible condition to help your children. It's not an admission of inadequacy, but a declaration that you have the wisdom and the courage to act, to do something positive toward

LATER BREAKUPS

Statistically, the trend is small but growing: divorce among long-married couples. Between 1980 and 1986, the number of American marriages that ended in divorce after lasting 25 years or more rose from 68,000 to 73,000.

In 1980, the proportion of divorced men in the group aged 55 to 64 was 5 percent. By 1988, that figure had climbed to 7 percent. For women of the same age group, the rates climbed from 7 percent in 1980 to 9 percent by 1988.

Sociologists offer various possible explanations. Some of these are:

- Older people are healthier and living longer.
- More people think they have a right to happiness and personal freedom.
- Women are getting more self-sufficient.
- Divorce doesn't carry the social stigma it used to.

When a long-term marriage breaks up, the husband is likely to be the initiator. Usually he leaves his wife for a younger woman. Typically, when the wife is the initiator, she has planned it for many years but has been waiting until the children were grown.

attaining healthy goals. Asking for help is a vital antidote to the terrible sense of isolation most divorcing people experience.

In writing this book, we have tried to bring a unique and varied approach to the subject of divorce recovery. One of us, Christine Archambault, is a co-founder and the current director of *Divorce Anonymous*, a self-help group dedicated to helping people survive the breakup of relationships. The other, Dr. Allan Adler, is both a psychiatrist and a divorce "survivor." Through his work at the Alvarado Parkway Institute, he has helped both men and women overcome the psychiatric conditions that sometimes complicate recovery from divorce.

Divorce therapy can take several forms: the support of informed and understanding friends, self-help groups, even professional therapy. There is a growing feeling among psychotherapists and others experienced in divorce work that group support, such as the support provided by *Divorce Anonymous* (which is modeled on the 12-step program of Alcoholics Anonymous—see page 113), may be especially effective. This group fosters personal insight, growth, and change, both through open discussion and through the empathy and encouragement of people who share a powerful bond of experience and feelings. No doubt about it, dealing with divorce does involve seeking out legal and financial advice. But that addresses only half of the issue—the "legal divorce." A strong, empathic support group is geared toward working on the other half—the "emotional divorce."

WHO NEEDS SUPPORT?

Support of some kind is needed for divorce recovery because of the *confusion* that comes with the pain of a dissolved relationship, and the sometimes overwhelming emotions for which the divorcing people are totally unprepared. Spouses who are in the process of splitting up may confuse these emotions with something else, or deal with them by denying them entirely.

Many divorced people look back after a few years and are astonished to identify some of the feelings which they had during the divorce but didn't recognize at the time. *Denial* is an inevitable part of the divorce process. Without realizing it, people deceive themselves about their own feelings—partly because the feelings are too powerful and threatening to be confronted, and partly because they need to protect themselves against guilt and loss of self-esteem. Many people are able to present a cheerful, brave front not only to others, but also to themselves. When friends offer condolences, they may reply, "It's the best thing that ever happened to me," or "I don't know why we waited so long." Both of these responses may contain much truth. However, they also conceal the deep hurt and grief that *everybody* feels during and immediately after a divorce, regardless of how much better off they may be eventually. Men, in particular, are likely to camouflage their emotional wounds. That's because in our culture "real men" aren't supposed to talk about what they're feeling.

Anger, another normal reaction in divorce, often gets denied or repressed. While some divorcing people may display their anger freely and volubly to anyone who will listen, others are burdened by a sense that anger is not socially acceptable, or doesn't fit their self-image. It's also possible that anger is an emotion they never learned to deal with. In far too many families, the expression of anger and resolution of conflict occur in destructive ways. A great many people grow up without acquiring effective ways of identifying anger, expressing it appropriately, and dealing with it productively. As a result, many divorcing people repress their anger because it frightens them. Others feel that for the sake of the children, or to keep peace in the house, or to avoid any appearance of unpleasantness, they must hide their anger and never express any criticism or complaint against their partner. Denial of anger, however, has its limits. Repressed anger may unexpectedly erupt in an uncontrolled and unmanageable form.

In fact, the denial or distortion of any of the negative emotions of divorce is likely to have important aftereffects. Some of these feelings may resurface later, at a time when they will seem bizarre because they aren't associated with anything that is happening currently. It may be difficult to identify them as delayed effects of the divorce. Denial of emotions may also aggravate the depression that usually accompanies divorce and the immediate post-divorce period.

Depression is one of the most common reactions to divorce, a reaction that both of the authors have experienced. A colleague of Dr. Adler's once experienced a serious depression after his divorce, so serious that he went to another psychiatrist for help. Later, when changing insurance companies, he ran into difficulty in getting new coverage because his record included a diagnosis of depression and a history of treatment for depression. "I wrote them a nasty letter saying that the *appropriate* response to divorce is depression, and the appropriate thing to do is to get help for it," he said.

Denial and depression take various forms. One person may withdraw into a shell, staying at home all the time except to go to work or shop for food. Another may suddenly become extraordinarily busy, making sure there's not a single idle moment in which an unpleasant thought might surface.

One great relief that can come from help, especially the help of others who are going through the same experience, is the discovery that your painful emotions (and your sometimes strange behavior) are essentially *normal* under the circumstances. In our age of "instant relief" from pills or psychological do-it-yourselfism, many people think emotions (at least troubling ones) are something to be "fixed." They think they should feel this way or that way, and they assume there's something wrong with being depressed or angry or frustrated. They find it difficult to accept their own feelings, and hard to imagine that other people feel the same way. Divorcing people in particular tend to think there's something wrong with them if they are depressed or angry or can't sleep. "Lots of people get divorced," they say. "Why can't I handle it as well as everybody else?"

In divorce support group sessions we have noticed that people's posture and expression—their "body language"—changes visibly when they hear other people tell their stories. "You mean I'm not losing my mind? I'm not the only person who goes through this?" The safe, comfortable environment of the support group liberates them. Suddenly they feel it's okay to think and talk about the fears they've been repressing so grimly.

The details of every divorce are different. In some cases there has been physical abuse or adultery; in others the marriage has "seemed perfect" until the very moment of the breakup. In some the property and custody battles grow unbelievably bitter; in others these processes proceed fairly smoothly. Yet sooner or later, all divorcing people experience virtually the same emotions.

Acknowledging negative feelings, and recognizing that they are appropriate to the moment, are important early steps toward adjustment to divorce.

Recognizing that you're only human, that nobody is perfect, and that there is a great commonality of human experience can bring a vitalizing release from guilt and anxiety. This welcome release enables you to deal with your emotions in healthy ways and to get on with recovery—to take an active part in getting over the divorce, rather than letting divorce be something that happens to you. Naturally, adjustment doesn't happen in a day. If you're like most recently divorced people, you have a tremendous need to do an "emotional postmortem" on the failed relationship, deciding what went wrong, how, and why. Completing this process satisfactorily can take many months. It's a good idea to take your time.

DIVORCE: A MIXED BAG OF EMOTIONS*

In the upheaval of divorce, emotions can run amok. Some of the feelings common to divorcing people everywhere are:

Humiliation: Feeling degraded for having "failed" at marriage or for having been "tossed aside"

Sense of loss: A need to grieve for the loss of your partner and your marriage

Disbelief: An inability to accept that the marriage is over

Desperation: Frustrating continued attempts to negotiate in order to save the marriage

Depression: A sense of failure and sadness as you acknowledge the impossibility of reconciliation

Ambivalence: Simultaneous feelings of loss and relief

Anger and hostility: At your partner, at society, at professionals who didn't save the marriage, at children and family

PRINCIPLES OF RECOVERY

A few general principles will help guide you through the recovery process; you'll read more about them in the coming chapters. In brief, these are the major areas on which to focus your energy:

Honesty. This means being honest with yourself first and with others as a result.

Abby, eighteen months after her husband moved out of the house, said, "I thought all I wanted in life was to please him. But when he wasn't around any more, I gradually started doing things the way I wanted to. In the short run, it helped me be members who take sides, and at everybody who "let this happen to you"; a desire to hurt and to take revenge

Guilt: Feeling at fault for the breakup, for hurting your partner and children, for "letting everybody down"

Euphoria: Relief and renewed energy after ending a painful or debilitating relationship

Withdrawal and numbness: Being overwhelmed by emotions and lifestyle changes; functioning on "automatic pilot" while you adjust

Desire to run or escape: Wanting to stop being responsible for yourself and others

Impatience: An urge to make decisions and changes quickly, to show everybody you're in charge and on top of the situation

Anxiety: Fear and panic about not being able to make it on your own.

*Adapted from "Divorce after 50," a publication of the American Association of Retired Persons.

straightforward with the lawyer. And in the long run, it made me a lot more open to other people."

A new identity outside marriage must be built on a solid foundation of self-evaluation, insight, and self-acceptance. If you're honest, discussions and negotiations will be less complicated, you'll feel less guilt and anxiety, and if there's a confrontation you'll disarm your opponent. Honesty simplifies life; lies create work. You always have to remember what lies you told so that you can tell the same story the next time. This clutters the mind, leaving less room for valuable thoughts. If you stay honest, you don't have to spend so much energy keeping track of everything.

Openmindedness. The ability to listen to others and actually hear what they are saying makes communication far more clear. Being able to talk things over with your partner and understand another point of view will greatly reduce conflict.

Bert, in the process of getting divorced, said, "I thought I knew exactly how she would react. I thought she'd get hyper about keeping the furniture and the silver. But what really happened was, she got hyper about finding a job and making money. Once I recognized that's where her anxiety lay, I was open to the idea of paying for her education as part of our settlement. It made negotiations a lot easier."

Openmindedness also means allowing yourself to examine and consider all the options that may be available, either in a given situation or in your future life as a whole. You may think you *have* to sell the house, for instance, or take a higher-paying job that you don't like because the job you really enjoy won't cover your expenses. However, it's possible you can keep both the house and the favorite job. Seek qualified advice, and be open to totally new ideas.

Forgiveness. Many people are hampered in their efforts to recover from divorce because they can't forgive their partner, but just as many are crippled by their inability to forgive themselves.

Claire, divorced for three years, said, "I still wake up in the mornings and think to myself, If only I had really thrown myself into gourmet cooking, he wouldn't have left me. If I had really been good at entertaining, he would have stuck around."

It helps to accept that both you and your partner are human, and that each of you, during the marriage, acted according to your own needs and feelings. Accepting responsibility for your actions is healthy. But blaming yourself too harshly is a form of self-dramatizing and self-pity that closes the door to discovery and growth.

Needs. It's essential to identify your basic needs, and to distinguish them from selfish "wants" and from what you think is "fair."

Neil, waiting for his divorce to become final, said, "I thought getting divorced wouldn't bother me so much if I threw myself into my work, so that's what I did. Then last weekend I went for a long bike ride, and it occurred to me this was the first 'fun' thing I'd done in six months. I realized I had been punishing myself."

It is *not* selfish to seek support for your emotional problems, to spend time healing your wounds, to seek some fun or recreational relief from the burdens of the divorce process. If you take care of yourself, you will be in a better position to help others—your children, for instance.

Health. Too many people neglect good nutrition, sleep, and exercise during a divorce. As a result, they are physically and emotionally unable to carry out necessary activities, and have no strength to deal with suffering.

Xenia, still in shock two months after her husband told her he wanted to split up, said, "I have to start taking care of myself. Ever since this whole thing came up, I've done nothing but eat. I've gained fifteen pounds. None of my clothes fit any more."

Roberta, a grade school teacher, said, "A lot of kids today don't take good care of themselves. They don't exercise, they don't sleep enough, they don't even brush their teeth. I think some of it's related to divorce. Half the kids in my class have divorced parents, and their home life is chaotic. The parents are so busy coping with shared custody, or hot dates, or whatever, that they don't teach the kids that old-fashioned stuff about basic hygiene. Believe me, it makes a difference."

Focus. It's important to recognize which are real issues and which are not. Money and custody too often become the battleground, when actually these are mere symbols of the deep emotional issues of the divorce. Lawyers and therapists are all too familiar with divorces in which big issues are dealt with comfortably, but negotiations break down over apparent trivialities such as who is going to get the exercise bicycle.

Harold, a fitness fanatic, said, "There is absolutely no reason why she should get that cycle. I always used it twice as much as she did. She's being totally pigheaded, and I'm not going to let her get away with it." The struggle over the cycle took weeks.

Structure. So many people in divorce feel lost or at loose ends, not knowing where to turn or what to do next.

Linda, facing divorce after a fifteen-year marriage, said, "I feel like a zombie since Bert moved out. There's no routine I have to stick to. There isn't even any reason to get up in the morning. Sometimes I don't get out of bed till noon."

Daily patterns of meals, work, social life, and personal relations form a kind of trellis on which emotional life grows. When these patterns are broken, it's hard to know in which direction to move. Consequently, it's important to erect new structures. At the simplest level this means ordering your day—setting aside certain periods for certain tasks, and for relaxation and escape, but not being so rigid that you feel imprisoned by routine. Keeping a journal of your feelings allows you to see patterns. Gradually you will see which of the things you do during the day make you feel better, and which make you feel worse.

Priorities. At best, divorce is a complicated process that involves innumerable practical and emotional issues. These can't all be resolved simultaneously.

Dan, whose wife was leaving him, said, "I'm having a lot of trouble getting to sleep at night. As soon as I lie down, my mind fills with thoughts of what I have to do to get this divorce. There's the whole issue of finding the right lawyer. There are a pile of financial arrangements. There's looking for a place to live. There's finding a housekeeper so I can make a good case for getting custody of the kids. Then there are the little things: my daughter wants a phone for her birthday, my son wants me to take him to a ball game, my parents want to have the kids out for a visit during spring vacation. I lie awake half the night thinking about what I need to do, and what I already should have done.

Making lists of things to do helps set priorities. Everything on the list may not get done on the day planned, but if you work your way through the list in an orderly fashion, you'll take care of all the items in due time. When setting priorities, ask yourself, "Which problems or worries occur to me as soon as I lie down at night? Which ones keep running around in my head all day?" Attack these issues first.

Support. If your spouse was the one who initiated the divorce, your initial reaction is bound to be a feeling of utter rejection.

As Chuck said, "My wife wanted the divorce. She told me there was no other man. I thought, my God, this woman left me and went to live all by herself—to her that's better than living with me. That got very hard for me to handle."

Besides losing your spouse, you will probably lose at least a few friends when you divorce, and you may lose your extended family as well. Explore every avenue toward new friendships: people you meet at work or through joining a club, taking a course, going to church, or getting involved with community activities or local politics. But hold onto those friends and family members whose support you value most, and who are willing to stand by you if asked. Some of those old friends and in-laws may not want to turn their backs on you, even if it appears that way at first. Some may simply feel uncomfortable about how to behave toward you; it may be that they want to help and to stick by you, but don't know how. Talk to them, tell them your feelings and needs, ask if they are willing to help—and in what ways. Don't burn too many bridges; you may need to cross them later. Seek and accept support wherever you can find it. Remember that support can also mean therapy or involvement in a group (more about this in Chapter Seven).

Time. It took a long time for you to reach the point where you are now; it will take a proportionately long time to move to another point.

Julie, divorced for six months, said, "I keep waiting for everything to be all better. I keep waiting for the day when I'll say, 'Well, at least that's all behind me now.' But so far it hasn't happened. I still burst into tears over stupid little things."

How much time recovery will take depends on a number of factors, including these:

- Who initiated the divorce
- How attached you were to your spouse, both emotionally and financially
- The roles you assumed during your marriage, and the roles you perceive to be available to you now.
- Your feelings of self-worth
- The external pressures you have to deal with during the divorce
- Your emotional state before the divorce
- How much help and support you receive
- How much effort you are willing to make

Think of time as an ally, not an enemy. When life looks bleak, remind yourself that this pain will pass away in time. Sometimes it's helpful to accept that at a given moment or in a given situation you don't have to *do* anything except be patient.

Regrets. Nearly every divorcing person, at some point, regrets lost opportunities for happiness.

Ron, whose ex-wife was a musician, said, "I look back on all those weekends we couldn't go anywhere as a family because she had a concert to play. We missed out on so much. She robbed us of a normal life. When I look back, I feel tremendously cheated.

Many people feel considerable anger and grief over the "wasted" years of a marriage that falls apart. It may take an enormous effort—an act of faith, even—to accept the past as inevitable. Tell yourself the past was a necessary part of your growth and experience. Convince yourself that the past *is* past, and that accepting your past is an opportunity to learn and to become the best person you can be. It may seem hard to believe at first, but it's true.

Spirituality. Whether or not you are religious in the traditional sense, the upheaval of divorce is bound to affect what might best be called your spiritual life. From a philosophical standpoint, divorce is nothing less than a **spiritual crisis**. Certainly, it's a change in your lifestyle and a redefinition of your personal assets. But far beyond that, it's a radical shift in your sense of who you are and where you're headed. This spiritual crisis has enormous personal significance: how you weather it will largely determine the future course of your life.

No matter what the circumstances, divorce forces you to cope with stress and discomfort—not just for a day or two, but for months and perhaps years. You're overwhelmed at first. But gradually, as you confront and resolve each new problem to the best of your ability, you grow calmer, steadier, more focused. Over time, you realize that **you have vast, hidden reserves of internal strength**. If you were brought up within a religious tradition, you may identify this inner strength as your faith in God. If you're more comfortable with secular concepts, you may call it a belief in your own worth as an individual, or in the value, dignity, and resilience of the human spirit.

With patience and diligence, you can find ways to center your life around the deep inner resources you are discovering. This is the process of true divorce recovery: not merely living through the bad times, but tapping into an inner core of strength that can sustain and nourish you indefinitely.

Does it sound too good to be true? Take heart! Genuine recovery from divorce is not a pipe dream, but a living reality. Although it isn't an easy goal, you can attain it. What you will need is confidence—in yourself, and in your ability to see clearly and act decisively. Achieving and maintaining that confidence is what the rest of this book is all about.

2

꧁꧂꧁꧂꧁꧂꧁꧂꧁꧂꧁꧂꧁꧂꧁꧂꧁꧂꧁꧂꧁꧂

WHO ASKED FOR THIS DIVORCE (AND WHAT DIFFERENCE DOES IT MAKE)?

"I just don't believe that two people ever wake up one morning and simultaneously say 'We don't have anything to do today so let's get a divorce.'"

—Allan J. Adler, M.D.

A marriage ends in one of two basic ways. Either both spouses realize that the marriage has disintegrated, and the general feeling is, "Hey, this isn't working any more." Or else one of the partners says to the other, "I want out." Whichever way it happens, every divorce begins before the divorce, with *one* person deciding he or she has had enough. Almost invariably, *one* person makes the decision that it's time for action.

Divorce therapists think it's important to distinguish between the one who makes this decision and the one who hears the decision announced. "Dumpers" and "dumpees" are perhaps the most vivid but least attractive terms. Others are "divorce initiators" and "divorce acceptors," or "divorce seekers" and "divorce opposers." We prefer "initiator" and "noninitiator."

Whatever the terms, it makes an enormous difference to the emotional reaction and the process of recovery whether you are the one who actively sought the divorce or the one who accepted it or fought it.

Wavering About Divorce

The announcement "I want a divorce" doesn't always hit the other spouse like a bolt of lightning. It's possible for a couple to waver about breaking up, vacillating for a year or more before deciding they really do want a divorce. Perhaps the husband moves out of the house, but keeps coming back to mow the lawn, sealcoat the driveway, and fix the leak under the sink. Perhaps the wife says she wants a divorce, then starts feeling sentimental and changes her mind. Perhaps they've had separate apartments for two years, but still go to the shore together in July.

Going back to the relationship in fits and starts amounts to a weaning process. Often, it's only the divorce initiator who benefits. For instance, if the husband is the initiator, he already has his mind prepared for a breakup; he may even be ready to redefine their relationship as a friendship. His wife, however, doesn't have it so easy. If she never did think divorce was a good idea, then his occasional visits may give her false hopes that he will eventually come back and be faithful to her again.

THE IMMEDIATE EFFECTS OF DIVORCE INITIATION

In many cases, however, the clear announcement "I want a divorce" is a total surprise which pulls the rug out from under the noninitiator.

There are many reasons why initiating a divorce makes such a difference. The initiator will feel guilt rather than abandonment; control (a central issue in both marriage and divorce) rather than helplessness; anger rather than fear; and—at least initially—resentment rather than loss.

Most important of all, the initiator has already spent some time "working" on his or her feelings, strategies, and justifications. The noninitiator may be caught totally unsuspecting and unprepared.

The initiator may spend from two to five years consciously or unconsciously anticipating a break. Often this process begins with fantasizing about freedom, or growing more aware of the partner's shortcomings. At this point, it's still possible that talking about the problem or participating in marriage counseling will result in reconciliation. But the initiator who continues on this course eventually reaches a point of no return, past which reconciliation is virtually impossible.

Of course, a spouse may initiate divorce quite abruptly, without going through the long buildup period we've been describing. Annemarie made a snap decision to divorce her husband, a stockbroker, after he was arrested in an insider-trading scandal. "I had always assumed I was married to an honest man," she said. "Then, overnight, my life was shattered. I knew instantly that I had no intention of staying married to a criminal."

Or the decision to get a divorce may be a sudden, violent reaction to a "last straw" event such as spouse abuse, marital rape, or child abuse. In these cases, however, there may have been periodic episodes of violence for years.

Cecilia's husband had a drinking problem, and it was getting worse. She did her best to ignore the issue. One night, however, when he came home drunk and she complained, he beat her savagely. After a brief stay in the hospital, she called a lawyer to help her get a legal separation, then took the children and moved into a battered women's shelter. When she told her story, the other women living at the shelter could hardly believe she had acted so decisively after a single beating. Most had remained in an abusive marriage for years before seeking help. One, aged 70, had put up with beatings for 45 years. These women said fear for their lives, or for the lives of their children, had long kept them from seeking divorce.

If domestic violence or sexual abuse has affected you or your children, we refer you to the Resource Section at the end of this book, which includes a "Physical and Emotional Abuse" section.

DIVORCE "REHEARSAL"

The initiator who is trying on the idea of divorce eventually arrives at a stage of mental role playing: How would I raise the issue? What would I do next? When would I start dating again? For the first time in the marriage, the initiator may suggest taking separate vacations that year, or find excuses to spend some weekends away from the family. He may go out with a friend to look for an apartment; perhaps the friend doesn't even realize that the initiator is actually thinking about living alone.

Usually at this point initiators are not thinking about hard realities, such as how they are going to handle the emotional

SPOUSE ABUSE AND DIVORCE

Violence against women is increasing in the United States. Every day of the year, a woman is raped every six minutes, and a woman is beaten every 18 seconds. An estimated four million women are beaten by their husbands every year; one-and-a-half million of them are injured badly enough to need medical attention.

If a beaten or raped woman does *not* react by immediately ending the relationship, it's because complex psychological knots tie her to her abusive husband or boyfriend. The strands of these knots may include embarrassment, ignorance, fear, pride, religious scruples, and/or financial need.

Typically, family violence involves three phases. First comes a *buildup of tension*, as the husband gets increasingly edgy, tense, and violent. Then the tension climaxes in *violence:* the husband beats, whips, or otherwise injures his wife. Finally there is a *tender reconciliation*, in which the husband plies his wife with love, praise, and gifts so that she will "forgive and forget." Over time, unfortunately, the cycle of violence not only repeats itself, but also intensifies.

The woman who is married to an abuser, and who initiates a divorce, may justifiably fear for her life. Possible sources of help for her include: (1) friends; (2) religious institutions—church, synagogue, or other; (3) a victims' service agency (listed in the telephone book under city or county government); (4) a crisis intervention center; (5) a marriage counselor; (6) a battered women's shelter.

problems of the partner and the children. As the process continues, however, their thoughts become more real and more specific, and tension begins to build.

Psychologically, the initiator needs to build up a case against the partner. There are probably many positive things in the marriage; there has been a life together, a family, a history of events and celebrations, and many satisfactions. Against this, the initiator must mentally stack up the negatives—defects in the marriage, shortcomings in the partner, and a stockpile of slights, real or imagined. Precisely because it's necessary to have these complaints all prepared and intact when the break comes, the initiator is not likely to confront the partner with them so that they can be dealt with and corrected. The initiator needs all of this emotional ammunition to pull out and use when it finally comes to the point of saying, "I want to leave, and I'm not going to change my mind."

The preparatory period allows the initiator to rehearse and, at least partially, work through the mourning, guilt, and other stresses of starting the breakup. The initiator has time to rationalize or accept the inevitable guilt, and even to ponder such practical problems as, "How can I supportively tell my partner I want a divorce without her killing herself, killing me, or being angry and making me feel like a total rat?"

The initiator will have some very mixed feelings at this time. There will be a satisfying sense of being in control of the situation, and some degree of smugness in having a secret from the partner. The ego will be nicely fed by the thought that the partner will be caught off guard. At the same time, there will be considerable guilt. Although none of these issues will be satisfactorily resolved, the pre-divorce period does give the initiator a considerable head start on the emotional work of divorce. Thus, at least at this preliminary stage and probably for some time to come, divorce is easier on the "divorcer" than on the "divorcee."

Meanwhile, the noninitiator is unaware of what's going on, or prefers not to recognize it. Perhaps the noninitiator secretly hopes it will straighten itself out, or assumes that the nagging signs of discontent are just a phase or a temporary glitch in the marriage. Maybe he or she has even thought once or twice about being divorced, only to dismiss the idea or postpone any action.

THE MAIN EVENT

To the noninitiator, as we've said, the actual announcement may come as a devastating shock. A description we've heard over and over is that of "having the rug pulled out from under me." Noninitiators feel as if they are caught in an undertow. They want to say, "Wait a minute, let's talk about this. Where

VERY-SHORT-MARRIAGE SYNDROME

Mike and Edna lived together for six years. Finally they got married. Fifteen months after the wedding, they decided to divorce. Their friends were shocked and mystified. What was the explanation?

Both Mike and Edna had long been dissatisfied with certain aspects of their relationship. In getting married, they made a common mistake: assuming that marriage itself would smooth over the difficulties.

Because it's meant to be a lifetime commitment, marriage sometimes accentuates the problems in a relationship. Two people who were able to tolerate each other as long as they knew there was an "easy out" may begin to feel claustrophobic once they've sealed their relationship with marriage vows.

But was divorce really the right answer for Mike and Edna? Maybe so, maybe not. Like marriage, divorce may prove disappointing to two people who are searching to resolve *all* their interpersonal differences. Perfect, unbroken harmony is the stuff of fairy tales, not real life.

do you think you're going? How can you do this to me?" In one sudden, shocking moment, the noninitiator feels loss, anger, a tremendous blow to self-esteem, overpowering fear, hurt, and confusion.

Eventually, with help, the noninitiator can deal with these feelings. In the acute period, however, the initiator has the great advantage of being well advanced in emotional adjustment to the situation. There is a distinct disparity between where the two partners are emotionally. This makes discussion and negotiation difficult.

The noninitiator can certainly ask for time to get used to the idea, to talk it over with a close friend or advisor, to seek help and advice. It's possible that, with the specter of divorce actually looming, the spouses may be able to work out their differences. However, if the couple continue to live together during this period of adjustment, the initiator may build up resentment, impatience, and anger. Of course, this interferes with the noninitiator's attempts at adjustment. A trial separation could be the answer, but the noninitiator may feel this signifies a greater degree of acceptance than he or she wants to express.

THE NONINITIATOR: POSSIBLE REACTIONS

Let's assume, for a moment, that it's the husband who wants out of the marriage. If his announcement comes as a surprise, it plunges his wife into an emotional crisis. She's fearful and terribly anxious. She trusted this man, expected to spend the rest of her life with him—and now, literally overnight, she finds he is her adversary.

Debbie, who had been married for five years, was horrified to discover that her husband had emptied out their joint savings account, and borrowed a large sum on their joint homeowner's line of credit, just before asking her for a divorce.

Debbie didn't want to believe what was happening. At first she told herself she could patch up the marriage by sweet-talking her husband. She didn't much feel like sweet-talking him, though, because she had evidence that he was running around with other women. "I don't know what to think," she told a friend tearfully. "Is our marriage just ailing a little, or is it worse than that—am I trying to feed chicken soup to a corpse?"

Can our marriage be saved? It's the noninitiator who will spend time agonizing over this question. Unfortunately, if the initiator has already moved well beyond the point of wanting to "fix" the relationship, the answer will probably be no. Debbie bumped up against the cruel reality that, even with all the energy, initiative, and goodwill in the world, it isn't always possible for a wife to make her husband fall back in love with her.

How does divorce look and feel from the noninitiator's point of view? The spouse who is stunned by the sudden prospect of divorce may characterize her plight in one of the following ways:

- **The "Victim" Divorce.** The divorce initiator falls in love with someone else and leaves the marriage. The noninitiator, who is left behind, feels bitter and rejected, and may start plotting to get even.

- **The "Irresponsibility" Divorce.** The initiator, tired of marriage responsibilities, opts to regain the freedom of singlehood. This often happens when one or both partners married very young.

- **The "Midlife Crisis" Divorce.** Internal changes and confusion, due to the initiator's midlife crisis (and/or an affair), trigger an impulsive divorce.

    The spouse who has had some warning that divorce was in the air may see her situation in one of these ways:

- **The "Empty Nest" Divorce.** The children were the main focus of the marriage. Once they grew up and left home, there was no longer any real partnership.

- **The "Problem" Divorce.** One of the spouses has a severe, long-standing problem such as alcoholism, compulsive gambling, or an untreated emotional disturbance. The couple may have a long history of domestic violence.

- **The "Stepchildren Difficulties" Divorce.** Fully 60 percent of second marriages that include stepchildren end in divorce. The adjustment period usually turns out to be longer than anyone expected. In many cases the adults involved just don't have the coping tools to smooth out the rough spots.

At this raw, terribly painful stage, both partners are particularly at cross-purposes. The initiator wants the partner, friends, and family to validate all the reasons for the divorce. The noninitiator wants to bargain, to show the partner that divorce is crazy, to turn back the clock to that stage where reconciliation might still be a possibility.

THE DANGERS OF DENIAL

At this stage also, both partners may be engaging in serious *denial*. The initiator may deny guilt by refusing to recognize any responsibility for what went wrong with the marriage, and may also deny that the divorce will cause the other partner any pain. The noninitiator may also deny responsibility, but more significantly, is apt to deny the reality of the initiator's intentions: "This isn't really happening." "He'll change his mind." "She doesn't really mean it; she just wants to clear the air."

For both partners this may be psychologically necessary. Confronting massive reality at this stage is probably impossible; denial allows both partners some emotional breathing room. But this is merely a defensive and protective reaction; it does not lead to understanding, growth, or recovery. At this stage, the ideal situation would be for both partners to declare a cease-fire and get professional support, together or separately. Unfortunately, this is usually not what happens. Once the word "divorce" has been spoken seriously, a certain momentum builds. It's as if speaking the word makes it irreversible. From that point on, an invisible force impels both partners forward. In this early stage, there is no time or room to adjust comfortably and in a healthy way. The beginning work of recovery—for the initiator, coming to terms with guilt and responsibility; for the noninitiator, accepting the situation without bitterness or self-blame—often must wait for a calmer time.

All of this makes "the scene" or "the announcement" a crucial moment in the divorce process. Like first impressions, what happens when the word "separation" or "divorce" is spoken aloud for the first time can have a decisive effect on each partner's immediate feelings and long-term adjustment.

In some ways, it's surprising that anyone is ever shocked when a partner says, "I want a divorce." Good, solid, happy marriages normally don't fall apart in an instant. Anyone who's half-awake or has any common sense surely knows when things aren't going well—or so you would think.

It's rare that one partner announces a wish to divorce without having already done many things, deliberately or unconsciously, to prepare the way.

For example, the initiator becomes more "picky" about the partner's personal habits, more impatient with the little irritants that are overlooked or tolerated in a healthy marriage—the cap left off the toothpaste tube, the dirty socks on the floor, the hair curlers at the breakfast table. More subtle, but more serious, is emotional and often physical withdrawal: spending less time with the partner, having sex less often or perhaps not at all, noticeably not paying attention when the partner is talking. At some point, the initiator usually confides to a close friend that divorce is a possibility. This is a significant step, because a feeling that has been spoken aloud becomes more clearly defined, more real.

Rationally, it's hard to understand how a partner can overlook these trouble signs.

But that's reckoning without the powerful self-protective mechanism called denial. People believe what they want to believe, see what they want to see, and sweep the rest under the rug.

It's particularly cruel to the unsuspecting and surprised "victim" of a marital breakup when people undiplomatically comment afterward that "everybody else saw it coming."

Denial, like so many other inefficient self-protective mechanisms, exacts a heavy price. In the case of divorce, the price is being unprepared for the "moment of truth," and unequipped to handle it on an equal footing with the initiator. Over the longer term, the price is that the noninitiator has more recovery work to do, both immediately and in the future. If you were the noninitiator in your divorce, your first and simplest act must be to forgive yourself for not "seeing it coming." You must understand that it's very human to want to avoid confronting bad news and recognizing rejection. You need to eliminate blame from your thinking about the situation. Reassessing your own possible shortcomings in the marriage will be an appropriate task later on, when you have moved beyond the acute anger, resentment, and self-loathing you felt when you first realized your marriage was breaking up. It's not appropriate in the beginning. When you're trying to deal with shock, hurt, and the emotion-clouding practical difficulties of managing a divorce, you need to put self-criticism on the back burner.

GUIDELINES FOR PULLING THROUGH

Since every divorce is unique, it's impossible to formulate precise rules or write a script for the traumatic confrontation—the moment when the initiator finally tells the partner what has been going on all the time. If you're the initiator, you need to handle this announcement in a way that will minimize the damage to your partner and reduce the burden of your own guilt. If you're the noninitiator, your best protection is to stand still. Let the chaos of emotions you feel run their course, without acting on them, turning them against the initiator, or trying to get rid of them. The best way to deal with your emotions is to express them to a close and trusted friend, or, better still, a counselor or support group.

Both partners should keep in mind certain key words: *honesty, consideration, patience, flexibility, openmindedness*. It's good to express your feelings, but not in ways that hurt both your partner and yourself. It's good to be open, but not to pour out resentment, criticism, and blame with total lack of restraint. It's good to be honest, but not to throw caution to the winds. What happens at this moment may determine the whole course of the divorce. An explosion of hatred will make recovery needlessly difficult.

This is difficult advice to accept when you are angry, guilty, bitter, hurt, frightened, and confused. But divorce is difficult no matter what you do. Your goal is to survive by practicing damage control. Professional or group support, which can help provide this, is especially advisable if the opening scene suggests that what's yet to come is going to get nasty.

Keep reminding yourself that even if you can't turn the clock back to a happier time, you do have choices. For instance, if your living arrangement with your spouse has become unbearable, you can make other arrangements. If the new living quarters are physically less comfortable than what you're used to, so what? In time, you'll figure out something else. And meanwhile, you will have recovered your pride and a measure of control over your life. You'll gain confidence that, even if your marriage is falling apart, **you** will endure. By consciously and deliberately building up your faith in yourself, you'll be able to pull through even the worst of circumstances.

If you have not yet reached the point where you and your spouse confront the question of divorce, there is still time to prepare. If you have already passed this point, some understanding of what happened may help you deal with your feelings now, and accept and recover from the feelings you had at the time.

DON'T TORTURE YOURSELF—OR YOUR PARTNER

You're almost certain to ask yourself: Why didn't I see what was happening? Why didn't I do something about it? The initiator may say, "I knew I was doing things that would only make divorce inevitable; why didn't I stop and try to work things out?" The noninitiator may say, "How could I have been so blind and stupid? Why didn't I recognize there was a problem while there was still time to fix it?" Both of you may ask yourselves, "Why didn't he (she) understand why I felt the way I did? How could he (she) *do* this to me?"

That last question is a particularly unhelpful approach to the problem. Very often the initiator of a divorce did not set out to "do something" to the other partner, and was not motivated by a desire to destroy or even to hurt. It's natural to ascribe that kind of motivation to the person who is hurting you—but doing so is almost guaranteed to make divorce and recovery harder for both of you.

It may be that you won't find an answer to any of these questions until you're well into the recovery process. At some point, you may decide the answers don't matter as much as they did at first. With self-discovery and a reassessment of the marriage, you may find that the breakup was inevitable and that neither of you could have done anything much differently. In the beginning, though, it's difficult to be honest with yourself. It's hard to have insight into your own feelings, emotions, and motivations. It's unpleasant to confront your fears and needs, and to accept the reality of the divorce without trying to fix the blame.

Much of this work of self-recognition can be saved for later, *but it should be done eventually.* An important goal of recovery is to see the past as clearly and honestly as possible, and to accept it as something that can no longer be changed. It's enlightening to learn to differentiate between things that happened because of your own flaws and shortcomings, and things that happened because of you and your spouse's differing personalities and the situation you were in together. It's crucial to understand that people do the things they do because of what and where they are at the time. Once you have worked through these stages, you can accept the past, put it in proper perspective, take what it can teach you, and leave the rest behind.

THE BIG QUESTION

What do we tell the children? This is a paramount issue for divorcing parents. Advice is voluminous: Everybody will tell you how to handle it, and dozens of books offer guidance. Yet much of the advice and guidance is contradictory. Parents (or at least the initiator of the divorce) would be wise to talk about this with a knowledgeable and trusted person: a psychotherapist or psychiatric physician, a family physician, a member of the clergy, a lawyer friend (but not necessarily the lawyer who is going to handle the divorce), a skilled and empathetic school guidance counselor, or a friend who has been through a divorce and seemed to handle it well.

Some widely accepted rules are:

- Don't tell the children too early, before you have settled the basic issues with each other and before you can estimate a time for the actual separation. Don't wait until the very last minute, either. Children need time to adjust, but not so much time they feel as if they're sitting on a bomb with a slow fuse.

- Be gentle, honest, and calm. Don't say too much. Give the children a simple announcement and brief explanation and then wait for their questions.

- Don't have discussions about divorce issues in front of the children, especially if you are hostile toward each other. If both of you can be reasonable and show respect for each other, you can have family discussions about family issues.

- Don't encourage the children's inevitable fantasies that the divorce isn't really going to happen, or that if it does, you may one day get together again. It's tempting to try to soothe the children's fears in this way, but it's cruel to perpetuate these illusions if there is really no chance. It will eventually magnify the children's disappointment, and postpone the time when they must confront reality.

In this important first scene, as in every later stage, children must *not* become the focus of the divorce. It's not your quarrels over the children that caused you to break up; it was probably the failure of the marriage that made you quarrel over the children. A husband may feel that the wife has neglected him and put all her emotional effort into tending the children; a wife may resent that she had to spend so much time meeting the children's needs while he never took any responsibility. These things are *not* the children's fault. They are due to the parents' differences, inability to resolve power struggles, or unwillingness to recognize each other's needs.

You must respect your children's rights and feelings, but you mustn't expect them to make adult-style decisions. Very young children, for example, can't be expected to decide which parent they want to live with. You can listen to what they have to say about it, and ask them how they feel, but you can't simply say to them: "Choose." This confronts them with a conflict of love and loyalty that is entirely too great for them to handle.

WHAT HAPPENS WHEN ONE PARTNER HAS SECOND THOUGHTS?

It's rare, but it does happen: the initiator has a change of heart after the divorce process begins. How should the noninitiator react?

After five years of marriage, Fergus left Nikki for another woman. Once she got over the initial shock, Nikki began to resign herself to the idea of divorce. The marriage had been tense and unhappy for at least two years. She had known about the affair months before Fergus formally broke the news to her, and she was dissatisfied enough to feel that maybe divorce *was* the right answer.

Gathering her courage, Nikki began exploring her options. She switched to a better-paying job, found a lawyer she liked, and did some research on divorce mediation.

Then, the bombshell. Seven months after moving out, Fergus called up and invited her out to dinner. Over white wine and fillet of sole, he told her he thought he had made a mistake. He had called it quits with the other woman, he said, and he'd like to give their marriage another try. Would she have him back?

Dumbfounded, Nikki asked Fergus for time to think about it. The next few days were an emotional roller-coaster ride. At first she was touched; nostalgia for the romantic early days of their marriage overcame her, and she longed to recapture that magic time. Then she found out through the grapevine that in fact it was the other woman who had dumped Fergus.

Suddenly Fergus' longing for "another try" struck Nikki as insincere. Although she tried to tell herself that reconciliation was possible, the unpleasant thought kept recurring that she was Fergus's second choice—a safety, a backup, someone to run to if things didn't work out elsewhere.

For Ken and Roberta, married for 12 years, the situation was similar except that it was Roberta who left the marriage. Mesmerized by the bearded instructor of an evening course, she took the two children and moved in with the professor. Ken and Roberta got a legal separation, and divorce proceedings started.

But Roberta's romance was short-lived. Six months into the new relationship, the professor confessed to her that the kids were driving him up the wall, and suggested they keep separate apartments. Fierce arguments ensued, and Roberta panicked. She called Ken, told him she was leaving the professor, and asked if he would take her back.

Ken was overwrought. He was desperate to have the kids back, but he didn't know what to do with his bitterness and rage toward Roberta. She didn't really want *him,* he thought. She just wanted a place to live, and he was a convenient provider. He told his therapist, "It's like she's playing musical chairs. All of a sudden the music stops and she's got no chair nearby, so she comes running over to me."

What happened? Nikki ultimately refused to get back together with Fergus; they were divorced, and both of them subsequently remarried. But Ken, despite his inner turmoil, took back Roberta, and the two of them entered intensive therapy. Two years later, they were still together.

When a divorce initiator has second thoughts, the tables switch abruptly. Suddenly it's the noninitiator who has the power to make or break the marriage. While this might sound like a dream come true, those who have lived through it describe it as a deeply disturbing experience. Having gained some independence and emotional distance, the noninitiator *once again* feels the rug being pulled out from under him or her.

"He asked me to 'forgive and forget,'" Nikki said, "but I couldn't. It would have been the worst kind of humiliation. I'd have lost my self-respect."

"Roberta admitted she'd been totally in the wrong," Ken said. "When I suggested counseling for both of us, she agreed right away. I told myself, 'Maybe some good will come of this after all.' So even though I was aching with hurt and resentment, I told her she and the kids could come on home."

Whether or not to "take back" a divorce initiator who has a change of heart is a highly individual decision. Some factors to consider:

1. How satisfying was the marriage at its best? If you have wonderful memories of earlier days, you may be willing to give the marriage a second chance and try to recapture that lost harmony. On the other hand, if the marriage was a disappointment from the start, you'll probably feel little or no motivation to try again.

2. How strained was the marriage before the split? If your marriage had become a living hell, the breakup was probably a relief once the initial shock subsided. In this case, you'll be reluctant to give marriage another try. But if you were never dissatisfied with the marriage, and you suspect the initiator's decision to leave home was just an ill-considered impulse, you may be more inclined to take a second chance.

3. Are children involved? Children want and need both of their parents. When the future of a marriage is hanging in the balance, the presence of children can be a swing factor. Ken, mentioned above, was deeply angry with his wife for walking out on him. His decision to take Roberta back was largely influenced by his concern for the children, whom he loved deeply. However, it was only after both he and Roberta had been in marriage counseling for many months that he felt he had really made the right decision.

4. Are both of you willing to take therapy seriously? The divorce initiator who claims to have a change of heart should be willing, and even eager, to enter marriage counseling. A professional counselor, therapist, or mediator is the best person to help you re-negotiate the terms of your relationship. Both of you need to have the same level of commitment if the marriage is to last. It won't work out if you're the only one who takes therapy seriously.

Nikki, above, decided against a second try because she couldn't get Fergus to commit himself to long-term therapy. She said, "I suspected that he would move back in, go for counseling a few times, and then tell me, 'I'm happy. If you're not, then *you* go to therapy.'"

In the other couple, Ken agreed to get back together with Roberta and then start marriage counseling. Some other couples in this situation might choose to maintain their legal separation while undergoing intensive couples therapy. If it's financially practical, this approach can work very well. It minimizes the chance that the couple will quickly fall back into destructive behavior patterns.

Whatever your inclinations about giving marriage a second try, be sure you *talk it over* with a neutral third party before you make your decision. If you're already seeing a therapist with whom you're comfortable, you're in good shape. If not, you may want to seek out a compatible support group (for example, Al-Anon is excellent if your mate has a drinking or drug abuse problem). Of course, you always have the option of confiding in a trusted friend.

It's not that the therapist, the support group, or the friend will be able to tell you exactly what to do—ultimately, the decision is yours alone. But airing your doubts and fears with someone who's emotionally uninvolved will help you gain valuable *perspective* on your marriage and your mate. Then, whatever you decide, you'll know you've considered all the angles.

In this chapter we've focused on responding constructively to the immediate emotional trauma of the divorce announcement. Anyone who has gone through the experience has intimate knowledge of the emotional pain of divorce. In the next chapter, we'll discuss something that's often neglected until it's too late: the "business" of divorce.

3

ⱭⱭⱭⱭⱭⱭⱭⱭⱭⱭⱭⱭⱭⱭⱭⱭⱭⱭⱭ

THE "BUSINESS"
OF DIVORCE

The messiest divorces—creating the worst obstacles to healthy recovery—are those involving money battles.

It's not just because people care so much about money. Rather, money battles substitute for—and are symbolic of—underlying emotions that are too powerful and dangerous to acknowledge and deal with directly. That interpretation can help straighten out a lot of your thoughts and attitudes about the "money issues," and even make it easier to deal with these issues.

Why are legal and financial bloodshed typical of so many divorces? It helps to look at what lies beneath the surface of the madness. For example, why should a man whose net worth is estimated in the hundreds of millions of dollars conduct a costly, ugly, and very public battle with his wife over the ownership of a house worth only a million and a half? Why should another couple agree to all the basic terms of a settlement and then come to physical blows over who gets to keep the tropical fish tank?

SEPARATING MONEY FROM EMOTIONS

These fights are not really about houses or fish. They are about power, control, pride, and revenge. They are also about the relationship two people had while they were married, and the relationship they now have while divorcing. It may be exactly the same old relationship minus the love. Or it may be a relationship so new and strange that it frightens both spouses into irrational behavior.

Of course, money has its own reality. It matters whether a

divorced man is forced to pay so much alimony that he can never think of marrying again. It matters whether a divorced woman has to work two jobs and live cheaply while her husband has a comfortable new bachelor apartment. It matters whether a divorced mother has no time to fulfill her children's emotional needs, let alone her own.

These are the reasons that both men and women need information, guidance, and legal advice when division of money and property is an important part of the divorce process. The business of divorce requires business decisions, and that usually means business (and legal) expertise.

OBTAINING LEGAL HELP*

You will want to choose an attorney who:

- Has experience in matrimonial law
- Knows the current financial issues, laws, and regulations relevant to divorce
- Charges a fee that's within your budget
- Respects your values
- Can negotiate with your spouse's attorney, but will litigate in court if necessary
- Would be comfortable advising you if you also decide to seek divorce mediation

You may also want to try:

- Asking for referrals from recently divorced friends
- Consulting a lawyer referral service
- Finding out if the organization or union of which you're a member offers legal services
- Asking your local legal services organization for public legal assistance

---

DOING YOUR HOMEWORK

The number one complaint to the American Bar Association

is lack of communication between attorneys and clients. Sometimes it's the lawyer who's at fault. Other times, though, it's the client who makes the relationship needlessly difficult by failing to do any homework. Here are a few tips on getting started:

1. Choose your lawyer carefully. Months down the road, you'll start to feel panicky if you suspect your lawyer isn't doing a good job for you. Personal references are reassuring. Consult a divorced friend whose judgment you trust, and find out who that person's divorce lawyer was. You may want to choose the same one yourself.

2. Go to the library or a bookstore, and bring home as much information on divorce as you can get. Divorce laws differ from state to state, so find out which ones apply to you. Take the time to understand how the legal process works, and how long a divorce is likely to take in your state.

3. Read over the material in those books until you've really mastered it. The more you can demystify divorce for yourself, the more you'll feel you're in control. Be aware that phoning your lawyer to ask a simple question may cost you $75 to $100 in attorney's time!

NOT WHAT'S FAIR, BUT WHAT'S NEEDED

Business should be only business. If the financial field becomes the place where you conduct your psychological warfare, the emotional cost is likely to be greater than either you or your estranged spouse can afford. As in the violent and popular movie *The War of the Roses,* it can destroy you—not just financially, but also spiritually and morally. It can leave wounds that no amount of recovery work will heal completely.

One of the authors, Dr. Adler, discovered this crucial point during the course of a difficult divorce:

"Paradoxically, although my wife and I both had a lot of pain and distress and anger to deal with, we were able to separate that from the legal side and 'put on a business hat.' I said we had a choice; we could pay $50,000 to lawyers and let them do everything, or we could sit down and do most of it ourselves.

"We talked a little with the lawyers and learned about the up side and the down sides. After six meetings, we were able to

DIVORCE MEDIATORS

About ten years ago there arose a new approach to the settlement of divorce difficulties: *divorce mediation*. Through this process, couples negotiate some or all of the terms of their divorce with the aid of a third, neutral person called a mediator. Usually there are face-to-face meetings between the spouses and the mediator. Each spouse may also be consulting an attorney. Although the attorneys do not attend or contribute to the mediation, they may review the arrangements and agreements before anyone signs anything. The fundamental idea is to avoid the adversarial, win-or-lose situation that typically develops when a divorce is settled by attorneys for each spouse.

The mediator's role is to open up a discussion, encourage each spouse to be honest and accurate, reduce anger and hostility, gain both spouses' confidence in the impartiality of the process, and guide them toward constructive negotiation. The mediator helps the couple to set up an agenda of important issues to be settled, and to pare away trivial or emotionally overloaded issues. She guides them toward focusing on their major needs and objectives, and compromising on less essential ones. She smoothes the way toward sharing information (in contrast to attorneys, who advise divorcing clients to tell nothing). Finally, she may pressure a stubborn partner, or one with unrealistic expectations, into moving forward with the negotiations. She then draws up a written agreement and obtains the divorcing couple's assent to it.

make a business decision that we both agreed upon and that we have both stuck to. We didn't double-cross each other, despite some pressure from lawyers.

"But for those first five meetings we couldn't do it. We kept talking about what is *fair:* what's fair for her, what's fair for me. Back and forth we went, trying to figure out this crazy idea of what's fair. We were stuck.

"One day my 70-year-old father, a self-educated and streetwise immigrant from Romania, told me to stop asking her what was fair and start asking her what she *needed.*

Most divorce mediators are mental health professionals, mostly social workers and psychologists. Increasingly, attorneys are entering the field of divorce mediation—a welcome trend, suggesting that even some lawyers are uncomfortable coaching spouses in how to be adversaries.

Since the field is new, there are few statistics on how successful divorce mediation has been. In the few studies that have been done, most couples who used mediation considered the process satisfying—usually more satisfying than their experience with the legal system. In addition, there is evidence that people comply with a mediated agreement more closely than with attorney-guided settlements. That is, they're more apt to respect the arrangements for child support payments, child custody, and visitation rights. On average, a mediator charges about half to two-thirds of what an attorney would charge. In divorces that involve disputes over large amounts of money and property, the savings are probably even greater.

Divorce mediation is a cooperative, psychologically oriented approach, quite unlike a competitive and punitive attorney-negotiated settlement. Those who favor mediation are convinced that with this process families are emotionally better off, and get through the divorce with less pain and trauma. California law now *requires* couples who are disputing child custody to consult a divorce mediator before the trial is scheduled.

"When I reframed the question that way, we made the deal in about twenty minutes.

"What she needed was to get educated, to have some cash, to be financially independent. It was a little more than what I had been offering, but suddenly I could meet her needs financially *and* psychologically."

The key that opened the door for this couple was substituting the practical word "need" for the emotionally explosive word "fair." As sages are fond of pointing out, life itself is not fair. Neither is divorce, for either partner. To try to judge fairness is

MONEY: THINK GLOBALLY*

Accountants experienced in divorce settlements advise spouses who are splitting up to think broadmindedly when dividing their assets. These pointers can save both of you money and hassle:

1. Take your anger and hostility to a counselor or therapist. Accountants and lawyers are familiar with these emotions, but they're not trained to deal with them constructively.

2. At the outset, set your sights on a global settlement. Instead of dickering about the ownership of each and every item, make a blanket agreement that, for instance, the husband gets the business, boat, and dogs, while the wife gets the house, car, and jewelry.

3. Split the ownership of financial investments (such as stocks and bonds) without actually selling them.

4. If you have jointly owned income property, sell it and split the money. Or hire an independent appraiser, and let one spouse buy out the other.

*Michael Kaplan "A Divorce Settlement Should be a Business Deal," *Los Angeles Business Journal*, March 13, 1989.

to open up the gate to power struggles, hurt pride, anger, resentment, and disappointment, and to use financial negotiations in a futile and hurtful attempt to fix the blame for the failed marriage.

NEVER USE DIVORCE TO "GET EVEN"

Unfortunately, in divorce, many men do try to cheat their wives out of what they really need financially, and many women try to take their husbands for all they've got. These people use the financial issues to get even and show the other person who's got the upper hand. As a result, many lawyers play on these unpleasant emotions to get the best "leverage" for their client. Of course, it's a lawyer's job to represent the client to the best of his or her ability. But far too often, divorcing people who, if left to their own devices, might have worked out a decent agreement, nevertheless end up in bitter court confrontations. This happens when lawyers advise them how to use emotional issues for financial gain—not just to protect justified and appropriate rights, but to win the financial war.

What exactly is leverage, in terms of divorce? One highly respected specialist in marital law describes leverage as pressure used to your own advantage, or withholding of what the other person wants in order to achieve your own ends. She advises women:

"To make the best use of all kinds of leverage, it's vital that your lawyer know as much as possible about your husband's behavior, personality, and finances. The opposite edge of the weapon makes it important that you conceal as much as possible from the other side—your deepest motives, desires, and insecurities in order to keep them from being used against you.

"It is a sad fact that the most decent people are often the least skilled in using leverage. They do not have the natural cunning to think in terms of turning others' weaknesses against them or to hide their own feelings and motives."*

This is a reasonable attorney who, without any malice or shiftiness, is giving what she feels is the best legal advice to divorcing women who need protection against their husbands. She assumes that the husband will take advantage of his wife's traditionally weaker position in both marriage and divorce. Her advice is probably relatively restrained, compared to what many lawyers will advise when trying to get the most impressive settlement for their clients.

Yet this supposedly sound, sensible advice runs counter to all the healthy attitudes and actions that can make divorce less traumatic for all involved. Anyone who exploits the partner's weakness will experience a divorce filled with guilt and unresolved anger, and will leave behind an ex-spouse whose initial indifference or mild dislike has been transformed into hatred. Neither partner is going to have much chance for a speedy and satisfying

*From *Getting Your Share*, by Lois Brenner and Robert Stein. New York: Crown, 1989, pp. 83–84.

new start in life when both are carrying with them that kind of emotional baggage.

DON'T FORGET COMMON SENSE AND DECENCY

Of course, it's a tall order to work your way through the very real complexities of a divorce settlement, protect your own interests (and those of your children), and also safeguard your immediate psychological adjustment and your future emotional health.

Your common sense and basic decency—if you can maintain them in the midst of chaos—are reliable guides and supports. You and your spouse should be at least moderately familiar with each other's financial situations and financial needs, and therefore able to recognize it when a lawyer is either being too greedy for you or else not adequately protecting you. Hopefully, if your lawyer is escalating bad feelings between you and your spouse into an all-out attack on the partner's financial position and emotional sensitivities, your good instincts will warn you that something's wrong.

ACCEPT THE FINANCIAL REALITY OF DIVORCE

Facing reality, as in so many other areas of the divorce recovery process, is particularly useful in the money department. Two can't live cheaper than one, as the old saying would have it, but it's obvious that two can live more cheaply together than they can apart. Maintaining two separate homes, duplicating furniture and necessary household goods, covering moving costs, and, in families with children, paying frequent travel costs for the noncustodial parent or the children—all of these can put a strain on resources that were adequate when the marriage and family were still intact. In most divorces, *at least in the early period,* neither partner lives as well as before. Unfortunately, women are generally much worse off after divorce than men. In fact, the wife may suffer financially while the husband gains a little, or even a lot.

It's healthier to accept the inevitable reduction in comfort and exert every effort to overcome it by your own efforts, rather than to fight against it. Unrealistic expectations make financial negotiations impossible. Emotional needs can distort your view of your financial needs. A lowering of your standard of living is a temporary accommodation that you can eventually find your way around. Is that the worst thing in the world?

Naturally, we're not suggesting that you let yourself be a doormat. If you accepted the traditional homemaker role for many years, trusting that your husband would always provide your financial support, you may have little or no job experience and absolutely no money of your own. In that case, the sudden prospect of divorce will probably throw you into a panic. What will become of you? How will you survive? Your divorce settlement must address these legitimate fears.

Make certain you don't give in to an inappropriate financial arrangement out of weakness or cowardice. But if you sincerely want to avoid bitterness and permanent hostility, accept financial reality rather than continuing to battle for an impractical ideal. It's healthier for the two of you to try to solve your financial problems cooperatively than for each of you to insist on being the one who comes out ahead. Remember to weigh the material losses of divorce against the great potential benefits of ending a painful marriage, rediscovering your self, making a fresh start, and discovering new dimensions to your life.

CREATIVE SOLUTIONS CAN WORK

Keeping an open mind and looking for your own solutions to problems—rather than copying the patterns of divorce settlement laid down by other people and by the media—can be liberating. It can set the scene for an emotionally easier divorce and a less stressful recovery. One example suggests how creative solving of the financial problem can be emotionally nourishing.

Kayla and Don had been married for more than twenty years, and had two teenage daughters. For at least five years their marriage had been emotionally bankrupt. They quarrelled bitterly and futilely over almost everything, particularly the children and money. Both spouses recognized that the family was in a hopeless state, but it was finally Kayla who decided that divorce (which neither of them liked) was better than the bleakness of the marriage.

Don hated the marriage too, but he was afraid of living alone and being without his family. His first reaction was to state flatly that they couldn't afford to get divorced. They were indeed not wealthy; they barely managed to live within their two incomes, without any extravagance. It seemed unlikely they could afford to live apart, especially since they were determined to send their two bright and academically enthusiastic daughters to college.

But once having confronted her feelings and made her decision, Kayla found it increasingly painful to continue with the marriage.

Finally she took a bold risk and proposed to Don that they separate. They would continue to own the house jointly (and share the proceeds when it was sold), but Kayla would live in it with the children. In return, she would take over *all* financial responsibility for the mortgage, insurance, and support of the children. He would have his salary and his small savings, intact and untouched, all to himself. She would make no financial demands on him.

In most cases this would make no sense. However, Don was about to retire on a fixed and not overly generous pension; Kayla was secure in her job and felt confident of opportunities to earn more. Eventually the couple did divorce on the terms Kayla proposed.

Afterward, there were years of financial struggle. Kayla worked extra jobs, skimped on expenditures for herself, handled all household upkeep and repairs, and with some help from scholarships, sent both daughters to college.

"There were times," she said later, "when I felt money worries were going to destroy me. But I gained strength from reminding myself that Don and I had separated without financial bitterness. I had no burden of guilt over taking money from an ex-husband who didn't have much to spare, so I could sleep nights without worrying that he was suffering too much. Our daughters were being spared the nastiness of a long financial battle. They didn't need to be angry toward either of us for forcing a lopsided settlement.

"Most importantly, I was earning not only financial self-sufficiency but emotional independence as well. I discovered talents and strengths I didn't know I had. When my first daughter graduated from college, I was bursting with pride, not only for her but for myself.

"And Don and I attended that graduation together, amicably and comfortably."

This case departs drastically from the typical divorce settlement. But it underscores the point that every divorce is different, and the "usual" way of settling a divorce is not always the best way. *This* solution was appropriate for *this* couple. It enabled both of them to leave the marriage with a minimum of emotional and financial wounds.

Throughout the financial thinking and negotiations, it's crucial to ask yourself at every turn: Is this arrangement right for *me?* Will it hurt either my partner or me more than necessary? Will I gain from it more than I will lose?

Openmindedness and flexibility in making a settlement are not just emotionally healthy; they can actually improve your negotiating position.

For example, lawyers often advise clients that when they make certain demands, they should also be prepared to make certain well-defined concessions. The concessions must be substantial enough to count, but not so great that they sacrifice your most vital concerns. Your readiness to make *some* concessions relieves your estranged spouse of the sense of being run over by a tank or colliding with a brick wall. Stonewalling, refusing to budge an inch, inevitably produces a counterreaction of anger and stubbornness. At this point, your firmness has backfired. Ask yourself: Am I going to fight for $50 a month more in child support, if it makes him so mad he signs the agreement while secretly resolving to pay late or not at all? Ask yourself: Am I going to take a hard line against $50 a month more, if it makes her so mad that she will poison the children's minds against me?

REMEMBER, YOU MAKE THE DECISIONS

Once you decide you prefer to be reasonable rather than turn the divorce process into another Vietnam War, it's essential that your legal and financial advisors understand this and agree to it. You must make it plain to them that you will accept their guidance about the legalities involved, and rely on their analysis of the financial problems and potentials. You want their advice on complexities and details you have no way of even guessing at: whether you should close joint accounts before the divorce, whether sole ownership of the house will result in a huge tax bill, whether child support payments or what is called "rehabilitative maintenance" will produce the best tax breaks.

But you will not allow them to use emotional manipulation to "win" the settlement. You will agree only to what's reasonable, not to what they think you can get away with through underhanded and divisive emotional tactics. The experience of many divorcing couples suggests that once a money war starts, everybody loses emotionally. The outcome is not victory but pain, regret, and a very sour taste in the mouth.

THINK OF A CLEAN BREAK

For certain aspects of a divorce, lawyers are essential, unless you are parting perfectly good friends and have no children, property, or assets to quarrel over. But lawyers are not psychologists. The emotional side of a divorce concerns them only insofar as the emotions can be used tactically in the legal fray. They can't be expected to pay as much attention to your long-term recovery as to your immediate monetary gains.

Unhappy situations between divorcing spouses often result from attorney-coached "no holds barred" and "take no prisoners" attitudes. Usually the attorneys are doing nothing immoral or reprehensible; they're just trying to protect and serve their clients. However, for your own peace of mind, it's important to remember that you know, better than your attorney, what your values and needs are. Only you, not your attorney, can determine how much guilt and self-reproach you want hanging over you when the legal maneuvering is done and you're finally alone with yourself.

When legal and financial negotiations begin to show the least sign of leading to battle, it's wise to get emotional support and guidance. This can help you clarify your own attitudes about the negotiations, and give you the backing you need to deal *your way* with the attorneys (who tend to intimidate almost everybody). Whether or not you enlist the support of a professional therapist, a good rule of thumb is to keep thinking of divorce as a *clean* break. At each step, ask yourself: How clean is it?

ENFORCED TOGETHERNESS

Psychological support is especially important in one agonizing and increasingly common situation: when spouses who want to divorce are forced to continue living together for months, or even years, before they can separate. Sometimes this potentially disastrous situation arises in response to recent laws, designed to protect the financial rights of the wife, which create trouble for the partner who actually "leaves the household." In other cases, the situation develops when a parent wants custody of the children and fears that moving out will weaken his or her claim to custody. More and more lawyers are insisting that their clients stay put, even when both partners have become so angry and embittered that they start fantasizing about "perfect murder."

Legal reasons for staying, or moving out, can be very complicated; no divorcing person should make any decision without getting competent advice. Ideally, however, that advice should include not only legal and financial guidance, but also understanding and support from a psychologist, marriage counselor, or other professional therapist. Like financial and legal support, good emotional support during divorce involves continuous cost-benefit analysis. You have to judge each potential "tactical gain" in terms of the emotional damage it could cause. You need to choose psychological growth, learning, and healing as overall goals.

Most divorced people who stayed together long after they initiated divorce proceedings will tell you that this unwanted togetherness was the worst part of splitting up. Being "married but not married" puts people in an emotional limbo where there are no rules, no guidelines, and no past experience or precedents to show them the way. Couples who begin their divorce trying to be civil may progress to pure hatred, maddened by the daily battles to draw boundary lines and resolve picky issues such as who sleeps where, who pays what bills, and who fixes the leaky faucet. Living together while divorcing amply demonstrates the truth of a wise old saying:

Most people can handle the major emotional dramas of life. What wears them down and tears them apart is that shoelace that breaks when they're late to catch a train.

4

♦♦♦♦♦♦♦♦♦♦♦♦♦♦♦♦♦

THE PAIN—AND THE GAIN—OF DIVORCE

In the Chinese language, which shows a rich understanding of life's complexities, the symbol for "danger" is the same as the symbol for "opportunity."

Divorce is a shock, a loss, a crisis, an ending. But it's also a transition, a chance for reawakening, and a new beginning.

It's not easy to see this second side of divorce when you're in pain. And there's no denying that divorce involves pain, sometimes at a seemingly intolerable level.

The pain is most acute and most difficult to deal with in the beginning. From then on, what kind of person you are and how you deal with pain will help determine how much pain you experience, and for how long.

Letting yourself get stuck in self-pity means prolonging your pain. But that's not the only choice that's open to you. Once you have sized up the past, you'll be better able to evaluate the here-and-now. You can decide what your personal options are, set realistic goals for yourself, and pursue them. That's called coping creatively with the pain of divorce. Moving ahead with your life won't make the pain disappear—but drawing on your inner resources will transform **you** and your self-image. As you start to feel stronger and more self-reliant, you'll focus less on pain, and more on gain. This is an excellent sign: it means you've succeeded in setting in motion the **dynamics of recovery**.

Whatever else it is, divorce is certainly a massive psychological and spiritual upheaval; afterward, you're literally not the same person you were before. During the transformation from pain to gain, you will pass through several stages: hurt at being a victim (or guilt at being a victimizer), a period of clinging to the past, anger at having to let go, gradual letting go, re–evaluation of your identity and responsibilities, and finally, acceptance of your new situation. Each of these stages offers opportunities for discovery and growth—so as you grope your way forward, trust yourself! As the old saying goes, "Have faith in your faith, and doubt your doubts."

Pay attention to your emotions and reactions as time passes. Periodically take stock to determine how far your recovery has progressed. Most important: if you find you haven't yet come as far as you'd have liked, forgive yourself— and trust that, with patience and persistence, you'll get where you're going. Remember, there are no set time limits. No one else is judging you or grading your performance. This divorce recovery is for **you**.

DIVORCE BY STAGES

To put it one way, there are several stages to divorce. Divorce experts themselves disagree about how many there are and what they constitute. Chronologically, you might say there are three stages:

1. The initial deciding-to-divorce stage, which involves shock and a great deal of raw pain;

2. The second stage, that of parting, in which you deal with the immediate practical work of divorce while beginning to find out what this divorce means to you emotionally;

3. The third stage, that of integration, in which you consolidate all you have learned, turn your face forward, and begin a new life. This stage may lead to and include remarriage or recoupling.

DIVORCE BY PHASES

Another perspective sees divorce in four phases—predecision, decision, mourning, and re-equilibration:

1. The initial, **predecision** phase involves achieving a measure of emotional detachment. Because of the shock and hurt, affection between you and your spouse is gone. Yet detachment doesn't come easily. One or both of you may fear living alone;

one or both may consider the looming economic difficulties insurmountable.

For many divorcing couples, the easiest route is to hang detachment on the hook of disillusionment. People who are dissatisfied with their marriage tend (usually wrongly) to look back and see the entire marriage as a failure and a disaster. Tension builds as the partners begin to look at each other and react to each other in new and more negative ways. Intimacy crumbles.

At this stage, unfortunately, both of you may shun counseling. The divorce initiator thinks there's nothing to discuss. The noninitiator fears that the very act of seeking out a therapist might confirm that there's a problem, making the possibility of an eventual divorce more real. Awkward attempts at reconciliation fail, leading to more disappointment.

Clifton knew his wife, Tiffany, had been seeing someone else. She had been open about it. Yet the first time she told him she thought they should divorce, he asked her to reconsider. It wasn't that he loved her so much he didn't want to let her go. It was just that they were so comfortable, so established. There were the apartment, the furniture, the cars, the friends, the relatives. . . . they had a nice setup. Maybe this was just a passing storm, Clifton thought. They began to "work on their marriage," doing the food shopping together, going on long evening walks, taking weekend trips to places they'd never been. By the end of four months, Clifton was feeling chronically irritated. He could tell that Tiffany's heart wasn't in it. She was just going through the motions. Clifton felt himself detaching from her emotionally. He was ready to talk about divorce.

2. Sooner or later, not only the private but also the public marriage disintegrates, as family, friends, and children are told. In the **decision** phase, when separation actually begins to happen, one or both partners may feel anxiety and even panic. Renewed attempts at reconciliation may occur, ending in new disappointments. Marital quarrels increase. Some couples go through this over and over before they finally accept divorce as inevitable. At some point within this phase, the painful discussions about financial arrangements and child custody begin.

Anita and Fred agreed to split up, but nothing happened easily or naturally. When Anita pushed Fred to hurry up and move out of the house, he suddenly got stubborn. After a month of searching, he claimed he couldn't find an apartment he could afford. Disgusted, Anita bought a camp bed at a garage sale and set it up in the basement. She told Fred he could sleep down there until he found a place of his own. Fred loathed the basement, and he loathed Anita for insisting that he sleep there. Humiliated and seething with resentment, he quickly made arrangements to move in with his brother. He told himself that he would agree to child support payments, but that Anita could forget about getting any alimony out of him.

3. Once the separation is accomplished, a long period of major adjustment begins. Single parents feel isolated and overwhelmed by responsibility. The partner who leaves home grieves for the lost home and family. This is a time of **mourning,** when people experience emotional pain, guilt, self-reproach, and anger.

Gayle kept telling herself that she hadn't tried hard enough. Why hadn't she pushed herself to learn water skiing and golf? If she had been more of a companion, John wouldn't have left her. "I always knew there was something wrong with me," she thought. "If I ever get involved with a man again, the same thing will probably happen." She dreaded coming home from work and wondering where the boys were. If John had stuck around, they wouldn't dare act so disobedient and wild. Periodically, she blames her parents for not having made her stick with college. Without a degree, she'd never earn enough to live comfortably. She felt old, unattractive, ineffectual, unwanted.

Mitch shoved the half-eaten cheeseburger away from him and lurched out of the fast-food joint, sickened. It was the fifth greasy dinner he'd eaten that week, and his whole system was rebelling. He had wanted the divorce, but he hadn't thought single life would be like this. He missed sitting down to dinner with the kids every night. He even missed Cassie standing up in her high chair and hurling her food on the floor. He wondered if his baby daughter would grow up hating him.

Ron set out cookies and soda on the coffee table. "Here you go, guys," he said. Jeff and his friend lunged for the food, and the soda bottle overturned. Two liters of cola were now soaking into the friend's sleeping bag, the pillow, and the carpet. Ron put his head in his hands. Nothing ever worked out right, not even a simple sleepover. Why had he ever pushed for custody of his son?

Once your first intense feelings subside, a more realistic and bearable sadness follows. After the divorce is final, this sadness slowly diminishes, like the sadness of any other mourning, as you begin channeling more energy into positive actions and feelings.

4. Finally you begin to **reequilibrate,** to find a new balance. This is a time of growth. Bit by bit, as you approach new relationships and activities more enthusiastically, the past falls into perspective.

Carolyn hummed a little tune as she pulled on her nylons and checked her hair in the mirror. After the divorce, she hadn't dated for two years. Now this fellow who had sold her the gas grill was taking a personal interest in her. She snapped her purse shut and gave herself a little smile in the mirror. It felt good to be wanted.

As Tim surveyed his class—five students who had come to him to learn kayaking—he couldn't suppress a grin of pleasure. Starting a wilderness training school was something he'd always dreamed of. Now, with the divorce behind him, it was becoming a reality. For the first time in many years, he was looking forward to the summer months.

The stages are loosely defined, and in addition, they may overlap. Sometimes you can't tell exactly what stage you're in. But if you stay alert to your feelings, moods, and behavior, you will begin to see changes and to take encouragement from each small bit of progress you make. There will come a day when you truly feel you can see light at the end of the tunnel.

PAIN THAT REQUIRES PROFESSIONAL HELP

Some people who are dealing with divorce manage to ride the emotional ups and downs with only friends and family for support. You should be aware, however, that the emotional pain of divorce occasionally gets out of hand. That's when it's time to seek professional help. Three broad categories of emotional difficulty—depression, substance abuse, and anxiety— are especially common among people going through a marital breakup. Let's take a brief look at each of these categories.

Major Depression

Feelings of deep sadness, unworthiness, and self-doubt are bound to arise as you sever a marriage that may have lasted for many years. But you should strongly consider consulting a physician if several of these symptoms of major depression describe the way you feel and act *every day:*

- Depressed or irritable mood
- Loss of interest or pleasure in everything
- Increased appetite and weight gain, or, conversely, decreased appetite and weight loss
- Inability to sleep, or, conversely, a need to sleep all the time
- Acting agitated or, conversely, acting unusually slowed down
- Persistent fatigue and loss of energy
- Feelings of guilt, worthlessness, or both
- Indecisiveness; inability to think and concentrate normally
- Recurrent thoughts of death or suicide

Major depression can be life-threatening; feelings of profound depression and hopelessness underlie most suicide attempts. If your reaction to divorce is deep, incapacitating depression, it's in your best interests to get competent treatment right away.

If you consult a psychiatrist, it's likely that your treatment will include both antidepressant medication and counseling. Perhaps you're wondering why you would need medication, if you're quite sure that your basic problem is psychological and is directly related to the divorce. The answer is that major depression, no matter how it starts, produces biochemical changes within your brain and nervous system. These chemical changes are what cause the *physical* symptoms of depression such as persistent appetite disturbance, sleep problems, and lack of concentration. Often, antidepressant medication can reverse the physical symptoms of depression within a few weeks or even days. Once you're feeling better physically, you will be more receptive to counseling. In turn, counseling can help improve your mood and brighten your outlook on life.

Alcohol and Drug Problems

If you find you're drinking more, or using more drugs or medications, since divorce entered your life, watch out: It's possible you're getting caught in the wheels of drug dependence. Please note that alcohol, whether it's beer, bourbon, or anything in between, is just another psychoactive drug (a substance people take to change the way they feel). So when we mention drugs, we're talking about alcoholic beverages as well as marijuana, tranquilizers, cocaine, crack, speed, heroin, and other "uppers" and "downers" available by prescription, over the counter, or in the street.

It's silly, and untrue, to say that divorce can actually cause alcoholism or drug dependence. After all, someone actively pours the drink, lights the joint, swallows the pill, snorts the powder. But of course, *something* does cause people to have alcohol and drug problems. Often the cause lies with a phenomenon known as *self-medication*.

When people suffer, they look for relief. Certain people, when they find themselves tense, nervous, and upset, are particularly satisfied with the relief they can get from psychoactive drugs. Initially, at least, drugs make them feel very good—competent, hopeful, "on top of the world"—and don't produce any negative effects. These are the people who, when faced with the multiple personal and social stresses of divorce, are most likely to go back to drugs again and again. Psychiatrists would say that they are "self-medicating."

Certain other people are distinctly unlikely to self-medicate. Some of these people have exceptional emotional stability even in the face of adversity. Others may experience ill effects, such as dizziness, sleepiness, flushing, vomiting, diarrhea, nausea, cramps, or headache, from even small amounts of alcohol or drugs. Susceptibility to alcohol and drug dependence seems to depend largely on a person's inborn biochemical constitution.

Unfortunately for those people who are deeply gratified by the feeling they get from psychoactive drugs, the more they use, the more likely they are to get hooked. Sooner or later, they begin to feel abnormal if they don't have a drug in their system all the time. Without even noticing it, they develop a regular drug habit. Since all psychoactive drugs are physically harmful when taken chronically, such people are guaranteed to suffer eventual ill effects from their drug use—including such heavy-duty ill effects as infection, liver damage, or brain damage. For the sake of their health, they need to confront and overcome their drug habit; the sooner, the better.

Don't delay. Seek help for alcohol or drug dependence right away if three or more of these criteria describe how you've been acting over a period of a month or more:

- Going on a binge (i.e., drinking or using more than you intended, or over a longer period than you intended)
- Feeling lousy if you go without; taking a drink or a drug to overcome the lousy feeling you get from going without
- Wanting to cut down, trying to cut down, but being unable to do so
- Spending a lot of time and energy getting your supply (i.e., theft), taking it (i.e., chain smoking), or recovering (i.e., hangover)
- Getting high to help get you through the day; or not showing up for work or a meeting because you're high or hung over
- Endangering others by being high (i.e., drunk driving, taking care of small children while drunk or high)
- Continuing use even though it causes physical distress (i.e., alcohol irritating a stomach ulcer) or psychological distress (i.e., arguments with others about how much you're using)
- Needing more than you used to need to feel an effect

If you suspect you have a drinking and/or drug problem, you may qualify for a medically supervised rehabilitation program. Ask your doctor. Many of these programs are excellent. Most guide you toward membership in Alcoholics Anonymous, or a similar self-help program, for continued support after you "graduate" from rehabilitation.

Anxiety Disorders

You've probably heard of agoraphobia. That's the condition in which a person suddenly feels deeply anxious, frightened, or panicky while she's in a supermarket, restaurant, auditorium, or other public place from which there seems to be no quick and easy escape. If the anxiety attacks persist, she may eventually grow afraid to leave home. Some people with agoraphobia become virtually housebound.

Agoraphobia is just one of several possible forms of *anxiety disorder*. Doctors still aren't sure exactly what biochemical changes within the brain and nervous system allow anxiety disorders to develop. What *is* certain is that divorce, with its attendant loss of social supports and disruption of important relationships, sometimes sets the stage for an anxiety disorder to develop.

Briefly, these are the common types of anxiety disorders that psychiatrists recognize:

- **Panic Disorder:** recurrent, unexpected panic attacks that last anywhere from a few minutes to several hours. Panic disorder can occur with or without agoraphobia.

- **Social Phobia:** an intense fear of humiliation or embarrassment in social situations, such as attending a party, speaking up at a meeting, giving a speech, or even using a public lavatory.

- **Simple Phobia:** deep, irrational fear of something that's probably harmless, such as a dog, cat, snake, fly, or mouse. Other "simple" phobias include fear of closed spaces, heights, air travel, and the sight of blood.

- **Obesssive-Compulsive Disorder:** either obsessions (recurrent, uncontrollable, unpleasant thoughts—about violence, for instance, or contamination by germs, or having unwittingly hurt someone in a traffic accident), or compulsions (repetitive, time-consuming, senseless behavior such as constant hand-washing, counting, or checking).

- **Post-Traumatic Stress Disorder:** vivid, intense reliving of a past trauma. Although this disorder is usually seen in survivors of rape, crashes, attacks, natural disasters, or other life-threatening events in which the victim was utterly helpless, a similar syndrome can develop in the wake of a particularly wrenching divorce. The person may experience flashbacks to violent arguments, and may struggle with nightmares, irritability, depression, guilt, fear of losing control, and self-defeating behavior.

All anxiety disorders are potentially crippling. If, in the wake of divorce, you find you're suffering from any of the symptoms just described, it's obvious that your pain has gone beyond the "ordinary" pain involved in splitting up. You should lose no time seeking professional help.

Fortunately, most anxiety disorders are highly treatable. If you go to a psychiatrist, it's likely you'll receive comprehensive therapy including medication, behavior modification exercises, and counseling. All three of these components work synergistically to unshackle you from the bonds of anxiety.

AFTER THE PAIN, THE GAIN

But pain is only half the story. Divorce also provides— even forces you into—many opportunities for discovery and growth.

To begin with, it jolts you out of your rut.

All of us develop patterns of behavior as we grow up and experience molds us. These habits become so much a part of us that they partly define who we are. When a shock like divorce comes along, we have to confront problems and situations we've never dealt with before. Sometimes the old habits work. Other times they're useless; if we keep relying on them, we'll be in trouble. Many old habits may have to be readjusted or even thrown away.

It can be like a snake shedding its skin. You only have to watch this happening once to know that it's a strenuous activity. But how sleek and smooth and beautiful the new skin can be!

You may be surprised when you take a look at the new skin. "I can actually take care of myself!" "I have a good sense of humor." "I always thought I was a coward, but I've been damned brave through this ordeal."

At the same time, you'll probably be surprised when you look back at the old skin. "I used to be terribly impatient." "Maybe I was a little selfish." "I didn't really *have* to interrupt my wife whenever she was telling a story."

EMOTIONAL POSTMORTEM

Practically everyone who is going through a divorce reaches a point of needing to look back and take stock. The first big question that occurs is, "How did I get here? How did I reach the point of divorce?" Other questions that follow include these:

- When did our marriage **really** start to unravel?
- Could this divorce have been predicted long ago?
- Why did I attract this particular person into my life in the first place, and what does that say about me?
- What's the real, underlying reason why our life together doesn't work any more?
- How, and why, did we stop being happy with each other?
- How much of the breakup was my spouse's fault, and how much was mine?
- What personal issues do I have to resolve to make sure I don't get into this situation again?

This process is what one of the authors, Chris Archambault, likes to call "doing an emotional postmortem" of the marriage. It won't get you and your spouse back together again, but it will help you settle in your own mind some of the issues the divorce raised. It helps if you can do some of your ruminating out loud, surrounded by supportive friends—another reason for seeking out, or starting, a divorced people's support group.

Hilda, for instance, said her marriage with Fabio had started to go downhill soon after they moved from Puerto Rico to New York. Friends in her support group pressed her for details. Why had Fabio been happier in Puerto Rico?

"I think it was because I never had a job there," Hilda replied. "When I came here, I got more independent, and he didn't like that." As she spoke, she realized that her independence was something she wouldn't want to give up. She had lost a husband, but she had gained a large measure of self-respect.

Christy had left and come back to Harold a half-dozen times before she finally made up her mind to get a divorce. She said she had kept returning to the relationship because she felt a close bond with her husband, even though he was openly unfaithful to her. People in the support group asked her how the bond had developed. "When we first met," she said, "I was very young and a little troubled. Harold was older, and in a sense he became my teacher. After I learned from him, I think he got bored with me. He went after someone else who was young and confused."

Her new friends remarked that her ex-husband sounded like a "rescuer," someone who gets his kicks from molding another person. Once the other person grows up, he distances himself because he has lost control. Christy was relieved that there was an explanation for what had happened to her. She had been feeling a lot of guilt even though *she* was the one who had been dropped. Suddenly she began to feel less guilty.

THE OPPOSITE OF LOVE IS...

Most people assume that the opposite of love is hate, but therapists know better. When ex-spouses hate each other, fight with each other, scream over the phone at each other, that's an indication that there's still a great deal of deep feeling between them. It isn't good feeling or positive feeling, but it's visceral. Their hatred shows that they're still struggling with the unresolved emotional issues that led them to seek a divorce.

The real opposite of love is indifference. When you finally reach the point where the thought of your ex-spouse no longer fills you with rage, or even annoyance, you'll know you have resolved those emotional issues. You'll know you have at last managed to free yourself from the hooks your ex-partner was once able to snag you with.

Betty had spent her married years in misery because no matter what she weighed, her husband never thought she was thin enough. After their divorce, she began allowing herself to eat whatever she pleased, whenever she pleased. One day, her ex-husband, speaking to her by phone about summer camp for their daughter, said, "I think she ought to go to a place where the meals aren't fattening. We don't want her to start having your problem." Betty surprised herself. A year earlier, she would have screamed at him to keep his cruel, vicious remarks to himself. But now, lightly and without any malice, she riposted, "Remember, keeping track of how much everybody weighs is *your* problem, not my problem." She realized that she was truly free from her old self-loathings. Food and body weight had ceased to be important issues for her. The divorce, she thought to herself, was complete.

NO ROOM FOR REGRETS

Dealing with the past is a big part of recovering. The ideal is to reach that point where you no longer dwell in the past, but don't have to shut the door on it entirely. You've really recovered if you no longer have to pretend the past never happened. Even though it was painful to live through, and painful to remember long after the divorce was final, the past can eventually become an integral part of who you are.

Too many people who divorce spend emotional energy uselessly regretting the "wasted years." A healthier approach is to take an inventory of the positive things that have emerged from those years, to identify the experiences from which you learned something. No years are wasted if they contributed anything to growth.

There are also bound to be parts of the past you wish you could rewrite. Looking back, you see not only things that hurt you, but also some things you did to others and wish you hadn't.

Once something is said it can't be unsaid. Once something is done it can't be undone. But it's never too late to do some repair work.

In 12-step programs, such as Alcoholics Anonymous and the new Divorce Anonymous modeled on AA, the ninth step is called "making amends." In simplest terms, this step consists of honestly assessing the harm you have done to another person, then telling that person that you recognize the harm you did. If you can make up for the damage, you do so. For example, if you have told a damaging lie about someone, you go back to those you told and correct the lie. If you cheated someone, you pay back the money.

A caution here: The ninth step advises making direct amends whenever possible, *except when to do so would injure someone*. Confessing past infidelities, for example, is usually *not* a productive way to make amends to your partner or ex-partner. In fact, it will probably abort any possibility of a future comfortable relationship. When you set out to make amends, be sensitive. Put yourself in the other person's shoes.

In making amends, it's crucial to focus on how you did harm, not why, and to keep the focus on what *you* did, not what the other person did to provoke you. There's no room for remarks such as, "I know I did this bad thing, but you goaded me into it," or "I did this, but only because you did that."

The "amends" discussion is not about the other person. In an important sense, it isn't even meant to benefit the other person. Usually the person to whom you make amends does get a pleasant, relieved feeling that justice has been done, and is very willing to confer forgiveness. But that's not the reason you make amends. The reason is to clarify your own view of yourself, to learn how to feel responsible (rather than guilty) for what you have done, and to cleanse yourself of the guilt you feel if you leave your own wrongdoing unacknowledged.

For divorced people, making amends has a special benefit: it's a way of finally "signing the emotional papers" on divorce, wiping the slate clean, and putting everything behind you so that you can truly begin again.

READY FOR SOMEONE NEW?

Particularly if you were the initiator of your divorce, one of the joys of being single again is the freedom to start a new relationship. Be forewarned, though, that it's possible to jump into this before you're ready, with unfortunate results.

Men, more than women, are apt to dive right into a new love affair on the heels of a divorce. What often happens is that the old problems, the ones that led to the divorce, start surfacing in the new relationship.

Ogden had divorced his first wife because he could never trust her. Even before the papers were signed, he was going out with someone new, and as soon as it was legally possible, he and Ilana got married. Ogden's happiness lasted about six months. Then he thought he began seeing signs that Ilana was running around on him. She denied it—first in hurt and amazement, then in indignation and anger. Within a year of being married, the couple started divorce proceedings.

Bill and his first wife got divorced because he fell in love with someone else. His new love didn't last, and Bill proceeded to become a "professional single"—a prolific dater. However, none of his new relationships developed into anything meaningful. Eventually Bill sought therapy, complaining of depression and anxiety.

Ogden's and Bill's cases are unfortunately typical. There are two main cultural reasons why divorced men are especially likely to get involved in a new relationship too soon:

1. Introspection is supposed to be for women, not men. Mulling over the divorce, trying to figure out where the relationship

soured, making time for sadness and grieving—many guys simply don't know how to do these things.

2. Traditionally, our American society orients men toward action. A man may feel a social obligation to pursue someone, whether he feels like it or not.

In our opinion, the social freedom to form new relationships *is* one of the gains of divorce, but it's not an unqualified blessing. Before you exercise this freedom, you have a responsibility to make sure your own emotional house is in order. And this warning, for the reasons just outlined, is especially important for men who often fall into this all too common trap.

5

⌘⌘⌘⌘⌘⌘⌘⌘⌘⌘⌘⌘⌘⌘⌘⌘

NEW RELATIONSHIPS FOR YOUR NEW SELF

"Seeing other people getting divorced is like looking into a goldfish bowl. When you get divorced, suddenly you're inside the goldfish bowl, seeing the bubbles and the gravel up close. Your sense of reality is completely distorted. Undergoing divorce means entering a new dimension."
— Christine Archambault

A woman who had divorced after more than twenty years of marriage recently encountered a man whose family had been the closest friends of her marriage. She had not seen him for about five years, during which time he had divorced and remarried.

"He introduced me to his new wife, and after only a couple of minutes I felt a tremendous rapport with her, a feeling that she and I could become wonderful friends if we had a chance.

"I went away from that meeting feeling sad, deprived, and full of regret. It was absolutely impossible for me to become friends with this woman or to renew my friendship with her husband, for whom I had once felt great fondness.

"The thing was that—typically, I guess—my husband had remained good friends with this man, and I had remained good friends with his ex-wife. To make matters even worse, my children remained good friends with the children of the first marriage, and my ex-husband and my children spent a great deal of time with these people. I couldn't possibly intrude into that situation.

"I hadn't really realized until then how painful the dissolution

63

of our friendship was. The first couple and their children had been like family. Our kids grew up together, we spent vacations together, holidays, celebrations. I hadn't felt so much loss since the divorce."

DIVORCE TEARS LIVES APART

This is what happens when people divorce. It may seem wrong, but it's inevitable. Divorce is not just a separation of two married people. It rips apart the whole social fabric of their lives—the complex interweaving of friends, families, children's friends, and even household pets.

Even if you're familiar with this type of disruption, having seen what happened to your friends when *they* got divorced, you're still likely to be shocked and dismayed when it happens to you.

Suddenly, your married friends may start to perceive you as a potential menace. One woman said, "I never thought of myself as a possible threat, but it's obvious to me that my best friend is uncomfortable when I'm with her and her husband. She suddenly becomes more openly affectionate toward him, more *possessive,* almost as if she were putting herself in front of him to guard him against me. There isn't even the remotest attraction between him and me. But it's almost as if I'm a symbol— the 'femme fatale,' or the 'dangerous divorcee,' or something ridiculous like that."

A divorced man says, "Nobody wants a third wheel. Sometimes I can go out with an old friend and his wife for dinner, but it's very, very rare. I believe about 95 percent of my social network changed after the breakup."

You're not the only one to be changed by your divorce. People around you change, too, in response to you. The results are bizarre and sometimes painful. One woman described the remarkable reaction of her mother to the divorce. Her mother wouldn't even speak to her. It was not because the daughter was getting a divorce, or even because she had been the one to initiate the divorce—the mother knew her daughter had been beaten up. The reason, it turned out, was that the mother hadn't had the same chance. She had lived within a bad marriage for many years, and suddenly she hated her daughter for having a second chance at making a life for herself. She cut her daughter off. The daughter didn't know what to do: "I'm divorcing my husband and also losing my mother."

OTHERS FEEL THREATENED

Although divorce is a loss much like a death in the family, the reaction of friends and families is by no means the same. When someone dies, they bring you a casserole; this is a symoblic gesture of closeness, sympathy, and willingness to help. When you get divorced, there are no casseroles. Your own close family may be there for you—but probably not your ex-spouse's family. Your friends may sympathize, but most of them don't know what to do. As a result, they usually take a couple of steps away from you. Some may confide that your divorce makes them nervous because their own marriage is on shaky ground. And even if they're not nervous, they may be embarrassed. Most couples have couple friends; now that you're not part of a couple anymore, your presence creates an awkward threesome.

In some rare cases, friends and divorcers can negotiate. One of the authors has a best friend who happens to be married to his ex-wife's best woman friend. Because they had many mutual acquaintances and friends, they were often invited to the same parties or other events, which none of them wanted to miss. They worked out a system of shifts. One couple would go to the party for the first two hours; the other for the last two—with a half-hour break so they wouldn't bump into each other. Flexibility and a willingness to negotiate can ease you through all sorts of divorce difficulties.

Most friends join a camp: his side, her side. Others stay away entirely because they don't want to take any side.

Sometimes this is preferable to the reaction of those who want to jump in and solve all your problems. Friends or family members may bombard you with advice, offering you their lawyer, their tax accountant, their therapist. In a misguided attempt to show their support and loyalty, they may not only agree with your complaints against your spouse but add to them, exaggerate them, or volunteer criticisms you hadn't even thought of. This only fuels your anger and resentment. Alternatively, they may moralize, asking you how you can possibly do this to the children. This just increases your burden of guilt.

The basic problem is that divorce represents a threat to everyone involved, in widening circles from the divorced couple out through family members, friends, and even beyond—

ultimately menacing the stability of society itself. This is true even in times like ours, when divorce is so very common.

MEDDLING BY RELATIVES AND FRIENDS

Another hidden danger during divorce is that friends and family members' behavior and reactions may strongly reinforce your own hidden (or not-so-hidden) wish to erase the whole divorce business and go back to where you were before. As we noted previously, one of the most significant issues in the recovery process is the completion of the "emotional divorce." When friends and family, with the best (or worst) of intentions, try to maneuver you and your spouse back together, they can seriously compromise your efforts to close the book on your marriage and open it on your future.

So you need to take stock of family and friends, and decide how you will deal with their behavior. Some friends should probably be pretty much excluded from your life, for your own good. Others you may wish to cling to—but if they don't share your wish, you may need to let them go out of your life both physically and emotionally.

TELLING FRIENDS HOW TO HELP

There may also be friends you want to keep and who want to stick by you, but whose manner of dealing with your divorce makes you uncomfortable. These include the ones who won't let the issue alone and insist on talking about it, even when you want a rest from it; those who hastily change the subject and never let you talk about it; those who pester you with advice and attention even when you want to be let alone; and those who somehow always seem to be busy when you call. If these really are good friends, and the trouble is that they simply don't know how to handle the situation, you may be able to talk to them about it honestly and directly.

Divorce counselors or therapists often recommend telling your friends what might be helpful. The idea is not only to smooth your relationship with the friends, but also to encourage you to take care of yourself. For many people, asking for help is a giant step. It seems to them that they're admitting failure and conceding that they can't make it on their own. It can be very liberating to say to a good friend, "It doesn't help me when you do this; could you please do that instead?" You're not demanding that your friend behave in a certain way; you're simply stating your needs.

Easy, helpful things you can ask of friends include: going to a movie, concert, or sports event with you (things you used to do with your partner and now can't face alone), talking on the phone with you when you're feeling isolated (not necessarily about the divorce, but about things you might have talked about in normal times), and expressing their own feelings honestly (saying, "I don't know what to say or how to handle this," or "I can be with you, but talking about your divorce makes me uncomfortable"). Most of all, what you need from friends and can ask them for is just to *be there* for you.

FACING THE RELATIVES

Dealing with relatives may be either an easier or a harder proposition. It's important not to set up specific expectations for their behavior, not to write scripts for them ahead of time. For many people, the anticipation of telling their parents or other close family members about a divorce is much more painful than the actual event. Quite often the family suspected something was going wrong, so that no one is really surprised by the news. Relatives may actually be more relieved than angry or disappointed. In any case, trying to imagine in advance what they will feel, say, or do will only cause you unnecessary grief.

Despite your long acquaintance with your relatives, you can't be sure they will react to any particular situation the way you want or expect them to. You'll need flexibility in relating to your family at this time. Try not to focus on exactly what they say and do, and whether you're disappointed by their specific behavior and attitudes. Instead, keep your mind on the basic issue, which is whether they're acting out of love, sympathy, and concern. If they are, the details are insignificant.

IN-LAWS: ARE THEY STILL YOUR RELATIVES?

Your spouse's family is apt to be a different story. If you make a clean and permanent break with them, at least the loss won't involve ongoing conflict and pain. But the break may not be clean. Your in-laws may not let you alone, even if that's what you'd prefer. Maybe they'll pressure you to come back, or to increase visiting privileges, or to let them take the children for a longer visit than you would prefer. In various ways they may "lean on you" on behalf of your partner, who is, after all, a member of their family.

In a surprising number of cases, divorced people maintain good relationships with their in-laws. A lot hinges on whether the relationship was good before the divorce. If you've been an accepted and genuine member of your spouse's family, the family ties may endure. During the divorce and immediately afterward, you would not want to visit your in-laws when your partner was going to be there. But later, if the divorce has been amicable, even this may be possible. When family feeling has been especially close, there is no reason for you not to keep participating in your in-laws' major get-togethers, such as weddings or funerals.

More often than you might think, members of the "other family" would like to keep up their relationship with you, would like to include you in these major events, but are reluctant to ask. They may be afraid their action could seem disloyal to their own relative. Or they may also fear your rejection. Whatever the case, if you genuinely wish to continue some kind of relationship with them, it will do no harm to try.

One woman related this story: "My husband's cousin, with whom we were very close, died a year or so after our divorce. I heard about it from one of my children, not my ex-husband. I immediately called the cousin's widow to tell her how sorry I was and to ask about the funeral arrangements.

"She was really surprised. She didn't think I would want to come. But she was really touched when she realized that I cared about her and about her late husband, and that the divorce had done nothing to change that feeling. She had wanted to ask me to come, but didn't have the courage.

"There are just times when other feelings and concerns and loyalties are more important than whether you still get along with the person you were married to."

A warning is needed here, however: Be sure you know your own motivations. If your behavior and attitude toward your ex-partner's family arises from genuine warmth and closeness to them, you can retain the connection as long as it still seems good and healthy. But if you cling to the connection because you have not really accepted the reality of the divorce, you will only complicate the work of "final separation" from your partner.

GETTING USED TO A "SPOUSE-IN-LAW"

Very shortly after Janine and Mark divorced, Mark remarried. The new wife was young, cute, and personable. Janine was crushed.

"They lived just across town," she said, "so she and I ran into each other fairly often. One day someone who noticed that both of us had the same last name asked me, 'Is she a relative of yours?' 'No!' I almost shouted. But when I thought about it, I saw that in a way she and I really were relatives. We had both said 'I do' to the same man. We were both involved in parenting the same children. We had the same in-laws."

The unwanted, but real, connection between Janine and her husband's new wife is sometimes called the "spouse-in-law" relationship. Author Ann Crytser would call the new woman Janine's wife-in-law.* These largely unacknowledged "in-law" relationships can take several forms:

If you're a woman, your spouse-in-law might be your ex-husband's new wife, or your current husband's ex-wife.

If you're a man, your spouse-in-law might be your ex-wife's new husband, or your current wife's ex-husband.

When you have a spouse-in-law, you are also that person's spouse-in-law. You certainly didn't choose each other, but you're stuck with the relationship. Like it or not, it's reciprocal.

Proper behavior between spouses-in-law isn't covered in any of the well-known etiquette books. Hardly anyone talks about this particular kind of relationship. Yet millions of adults across America have a spouse-in-law, and sometimes more than one.

Feelings between the old spouse and the new spouse are usually tense and bitter, at least initially.

Richard, a year and a half after his divorce, was starting to feel that the worst of the pain was behind him. Then he opened the local newspaper and recognized a wedding photo of his ex-wife, who had just remarried. "I saw that guy's face," he said, "and I

---

*Crytser, Ann: *The Wife-In-Law Trap*. Pocket Books, 1990.

wanted to kill him. I felt like I didn't exist any more—like he had stepped in and replaced me. And now I was going to have to send child support payments to this joker's house?"

Lisa despised sharing custody of her children with her ex-husband and his new wife, Barbara. Where Lisa was strict, Barbara was lax. Where Lisa was frugal, Barbara was lavish. Where Lisa stuck to regular mealtimes and bedtimes, Barbara operated without a schedule. Lisa felt Barbara was doing it on purpose to make her look like an ogre.

Of course, many divorced people find that their resentment of their ex-spouse's new partner fades when they themselves remarry. With or without remarriage, time will eventually heal many of the wounds that opened when you first acquired a spouse-in-law. But this process can't be rushed. Over the short term, it's best to accept that relating to a new spouse-in-law is never easy or natural. These suggestions may help:

- Avoid letting your children get caught in the crossfire.
- Try to understand your spouse-in-law's position, at least intellectually.
- Share your negative thoughts and feelings. Talk to a counselor, members of a support group, or good friends.
- Nurture yourself. Follow your own new interests. Avoid getting caught in the "victim" trap.
- Try to find some humor in your situation. Even if you don't feel like acting civil toward your spouse-in-law, do your best to fake it.

RECONNECTING WITH THE WORLD

Connections are hard to give up. But when you do give them up, you need new ones to take their place. After divorce, isolation is the enemy of growth and recovery. If you are working at self-knowledge and growth, new connections are your keys to learning different ways of relating to people. There are a number of important issues related to new connections:

- **Your own choices.** In your marriage, many of your friends may have been "couple" friends—people who were already friends of your husband or wife, who became friends only because they were neighbors or the parents of your children's friends, or who were business associates of your spouse. Some of these couples may have been "compromise" friends— chosen mostly because none of the four of you took a particular dislike to any of the others. (It isn't easy to find four friends who really like each other. Sometimes the husbands like each other even if the wives don't, or he likes the wife even if she can't stand the husband, or vice versa.) You may not have felt particularly close to any of these people. You might not have been friends with any of them if it weren't for your marriage.

Now you have the opportunity to find your own friends, and to choose them for the best reasons: because you have much in common, because you have shared values and interests, because you trust each other. You can begin to see other people for themselves and from your own viewpoint, not as part of a couple whose joint needs have to be negotiated in friendships.

■ **Your Own Person.** As you get used to being divorced, you rediscover yourself—or perhaps discover yourself for the first time. Once you've established a solid relationship with yourself, you're ready to relate creatively to others. At this point, in meeting other people you have a better chance to learn your own value as an individual and to risk being truly yourself, rather than trying to fit into the role of "wife" or "husband" or the person your partner wanted you to be.

■ **Your Own Needs.** Too often, in their relationships with friends as well as in their relationships with each other, married people find themselves putting on an act to "please" their partner or live up to the partner's expectations.

"My wife liked to give these big formal dinner parties where she could show off the house and her cooking and my business success. I knew it was important to her, but I would rather have had a barbecue."

"My husband was a macho intellectual. He liked to exercise power by showing off how much he knew. When we were with friends or family, my role was to be the wide-eyed listener, totally awed by his mind and his talk. The thing is, I bought it. I really thought that compared to him I wasn't very bright. So I fed him his lines and backed up his opinions, and it wasn't until after we divorced that I realized I really have a mind of my own. Maybe even better than his."

Many people do not marry people, but "concepts." They choose a partner who seems to fit the role they have imagined a partner should fill: "the little woman" or "the good provider"; the wife who is "a lady in public and a wanton in bed"; the husband who will reinforce his wife's glamorous self-image by "showing her off" to his friends. Even if they don't exactly fit their roles, they try to play them fully, often subduing their own genuine natures.

Divorce provides an opportunity to rediscover yourself, to find out whether you really are that person you have been playing all this time. Because you have nothing to lose in making new friendships and new relationships, you can dare to be exactly who you find that you are.

■ **Your Own "Aloneness."** Being alone does not need to mean being lonely. In fact, as we saw in Chapter Four, it's usually a mistake to react to divorce by jumping immediately into a new intimate relationship. In the aftermath of divorce, make sure you know the difference between aloneness and loneliness. Value your private and quiet time, but don't get stuck in it, letting privacy turn into alienation. Having some connectedness with the rest of humanity is as vital to life as food and water.

DATING IS NOT A GAME

At some point, new relationships will mean dating. This is an area as full of pitfalls as of promise, and there are few rules to guide you. Some people begin dating immediately; others never do. One divorced woman said:

"I am 49 years old. My husband and I met in junior high and were high school sweethearts, and I never dated anyone else. We married right out of high school. Now at my age I'm supposed to go out on a date? You've got to be kidding. My life is over."

A divorced man said:

"I knew what my needs were, so I started marketing myself as a divorced man very quickly and very consciously. I like the special intimacy I feel with women. So I started dating almost before the divorce was over, and I've been dating ever since."

Some people would like to begin dating but don't know how. Others never meet anybody who is suitable. For people in their forties and fifties, the choices are limited; every new person they meet is either married already or never was "marriage material" to begin with. Apart from these problems, many divorced people have trouble resuming relationships with the opposite sex because of unhealthy attitudes and fears. Some examples of post-divorce "wrongthink":

Who Would Want to Go Out with a Loser Like Me? This harks back to the idea that divorce is a failure and that a divorced person is somebody who "couldn't make it" in marriage. Self-discovery and reevaluation of yourself *as an individual,* without reference to your marriage or divorce, can help you come to recognize yourself as a worthwhile person, someone who has much to offer, even somebody that "anyone would be lucky to get a date with."

I'm Not Ready for Another Commitment. If you fear that dating may lead the date to think you're ready for something more permanent, you're out of touch with the prevailing feelings and trends in today's relationships. Many people are wary of commitment. Others are open to it, but don't expect it to result from the very next date. Lots of people date simply because they enjoy the company of the opposite sex or want to enrich their lives with new associations.

I Don't Want to Get Hurt Again. If you're not looking for an instant replacement for your ex-partner; if you're growing and developing beyond the immature impulse to fall in love at every possible opportunity; if your marriage and divorce experience has given you insight into your own needs and understanding of other people's needs—then you're in no more danger of getting hurt now than anybody else is. It's true that in romance, people sometimes get hurt. If you're really recovering, you can take the risk—and even get hurt—without being destroyed by it. If you're still at the very beginning of recovery, and haven't yet developed new ways of relating to other people, dating right now might indeed be a danger. Let it wait until you have "practiced" on nonromantic friendships.

I'm Too Old. The change in people's attitudes toward age today is almost as remarkable—if not as visible—as the changed status of women or the changed attitudes toward sexuality. This is true even for older women. Not so long ago, older men were considered more attractive than older women, despite equal degrees of white hair and wrinkles. Fortunately, this attitude is disappearing. It's helpful to remember that age 65 was *arbitrarily* chosen as a definition of "old," purely and simply to provide a baseline age for the Social Security Act of 1939. Age is "a state of mind" or "a crisis of the imagination." You really *are* only as old as you feel.

Older people have valuable experience to offer in a new relationship—perhaps especially so if they have been divorced, and have matured through the process of recovery.

START SLOWLY

One way to overcome fear of dating is to begin with "safe dates": nonintimate engagements for a concert, a lecture, or a sporting event with someone whom you know well and who will share your assumption that romance is not on the agenda. Once you have succeeded in this nonthreatening experiment, you may find the courage to venture into more rapid currents.

Whether you're male or female, there is no reason to avoid dating someone younger or older than yourself. People whose company you will value are not going to have narrow, prejudiced attitudes toward age differences. When you've reached the point in your recovery from divorce where you're secure in who you are and how attractive you are as a human being, you'll be able to trust that someone else can see those same things. You'll realize that the ideal male and female aren't necessarily an iron-pumper and Miss America. Those are just commercial concepts. They don't define beauty for you, or for anyone else in particular! You may even to able to stop looking with dismay at the calendar of years or your image in the mirror, and instead start seeing yourself from the inside, as people with real sensitivity and emotional maturity will do.

Dating may seem like an adventure or a danger. It may be something you feel driven to do out of loneliness or sexual need. It may be something you shy away from for all the reasons mentioned in this chapter, or because of other fears. Most divorced people, however, should consider dating to be one of their goals for recovery. Starting to date again can be not only a sign of a return to emotional health, but also an opportunity to enhance that process.

THE NEXT STEP: INTIMACY

So you've found someone with whom you really click. First comes dating, then comes intimacy. Or does it?

If your divorce is still haunting you, you may be very reluctant to let a new relationship get as far as intimacy. As long as you can keep your date at a safe psychological distance, you're sure you won't get entangled in anything like the emotional jungle of your former marriage.

Sooner or later, however, you'll probably hunger for something deeper than just casual friendship. At that point, you'll bump right into the issue of intimacy. Let's take a better look. What is intimacy, anyway?

It's not simply a synonym for having sex together. Nor does it mean being together and doing everything together twenty-four hours a day. Rather, intimacy means being emotionally close. It means living day in, day out with a mutual sense of acceptance and trust. It means *being there* for each other without either person stifling or smothering the other.

Sounds good—and simple. Why do people have such a hard time achieving and maintaining intimacy?

As Eileen McCann explains it in *The Two-Step,** people struggle with intimacy because they believe that only through union with someone else can they be whole. But this is really a myth. If you're honest with yourself you'll admit that, just like everybody else, you are basically alone in the world. No one else will ever really know exactly what your own experiences are—neither your fantasies, dreams, and orgasms nor your needs, sorrows, and pains.

Within a relationship, then, accepting your own aloneness is a major step. It means you no longer look to the other person to complete you and make you whole. Instead, you and the partner with whom you are intimate constantly shift back and forth between the two basic roles of *seeker* and *sought*. Instead of one of you doing all the giving, and the other doing all the

*Eileen McCann and Douglas Shannon (illustrator): *The Two-Step*. Grove Press, 1985.

receiving, both of you switch frequently. This makes the relationship alive and vital, instead of dead and stifling.

Of course, it's hard to switch out of a comfortable, familiar role. If you're used to being the one who initiates and pursues, who organizes and makes things happen, it will be hard for you to sit back and wait for your partner to take the initiative sometimes. And if you're accustomed to being the one who sits tight, sets limits, and defends your territory and your privacy, it will be hard for you to take those first steps toward deciding what you want and going after it. In either case, you'll be scared that the partner won't make the switch in synch with you—and that you'll be left high and dry without a partner.

For both of you, the crucial point is to *share* with each other your fears of loss and surrender. By exposing your vulnerabilities to each other in a spirit of trust and acceptance, you and your partner will gradually move toward intimacy—that state of seeing each other, being seen by each other, and intending to go on living life that way.

It isn't easy. Intimacy involves real risks for both partners, and real commitment. But since the dividends are joy and a renewed sense of meaning and purpose in life, striving toward intimacy is well worth the effort.

6

༺༺༺༺༺༺༺༺༺༺༺༺༺༺

THE ONLY INNOCENT VICTIMS

Every year, in the United States, divorce and child custody disputes affect more than 1,200,000 families—that's one *million*, two hundred thousand. How many children?

Psychologists agree that the divorce process is always traumatic for children, at least temporarily and sometimes permanently. Children are the innocent victims of divorce.

Psychologists sometimes say, "There are no victims, only volunteers." What they mean is that regardless of the influences that may have molded any individual's nature, that person has a will and can exercise a certain amount of initiative to avoid or escape from victimizing circumstances.

One woman put it succinctly. When her husband complained that the divorce was her fault, because she "took over everything" and wouldn't let him have any say in big issues such as money or the children, she retorted, "And where were you while all this was happening to you?"

There are two sides to every divorce. Even in cases where one spouse has obviously been a bully, an abuser, or a tyrant, the other can't be called "a victim" in the sense of being totally powerless against the aggressor.

Children are a different matter.

No matter how much trouble they may have caused, no matter to what extent they were the focus or the trigger for marital battles, children are *never* the "cause" of divorce. They are always its victims. Children are powerless to alter or escape the pain of an unhappy marriage or of divorce. They're stuck with the parents they've got.

BETTER OFF—IN WHAT WAYS?

In general, psychologists accept the old saying that it's better for the children when unhappy parents divorce than when they continue to poison the home atmosphere with bitterness or violence. But this doesn't mean that divorce leaves children unscathed. Consider the following:

- Over a three-year period, children in general run a 26 percent risk of developing health problems. Among children of divorced or separated parents, the risk is 35 percent. Almost one-third of the illnesses are tonsillitis, ear infections, or pneumonia; other problems are allergies, asthma, chronic lung problems, skin conditions, and urinary infections.

- Even when the mother remarries, the children's higher illness rate persists, and in fact *increases* after the first four years of family separation.

- For many children, divorce means the end of health insurance. It may also mean the loss of such advantages as a safe, comfortable environment, good food, and constant adult supervision. Forty-one percent of divorced mothers receive no child support payments at all. Those who do usually collect only 70 percent of what they are due.

- Preteens and teens who enter treatment programs for alcohol and drug abuse are overwhelmingly children of divorce.

- Most young people ages 14–24 who attempt or actually commit suicide are the sons and daughters of the divorced.

Realistically, the issue isn't "*Are* the children going to get hurt?" but "*How much* are they going to get hurt?" The issue isn't *whether* you can continue to share the parenthood of your children, but *how* you are going to do it in the new circumstances of divorce.

The answers are entirely up to the two of you. When it comes to the children, both of you must think of yourselves as parents, not as husband and wife or ex-husband and ex-wife.

Volumes of material have been written about the children of divorce. Much of the information is contradictory. However, virtually everyone who has experienced divorce and its effects on children agree on one point: *The major source of children's psychological distress is conflict during the divorce settlement and continued conflict following the divorce.* Ill effects on children aren't confined to the actual period of divorce; nervousness over the parents' quarrels before the marital breakup may progress to feelings of abandonment as a result of custody arrangements.

The moral: For the children's sake, negotiate.

LEARNING THE ART OF NEGOTIATION

Negotiation in this context applies not just to the legal maneuvering of money settlement and child custody, but to all your actions—from the initiation of the divorce, through the years of custody, until the children are independent adults. You and your spouse *can* cooperate on all these negotiations if you're willing to put your children's welfare before your own anger. Despite what you might think, parents can work together even if they don't like each other.

It begins with announcing the divorce to the children. In this area, there's considerable agreement among the experts on how to proceed. This is a representative example:

Once it's apparent that separation and divorce are inevitable, discuss the issues with the children to prepare them for the actual event, keeping in mind their ages and stages of development. Ideally, with preschool children, this should happen about a week or two before the planned separation; with older children, as early as possible. Of course, divorce is often a crisis that doesn't allow time for lots of advance notice to the children. Just do the best you can.

Second, talk to the children—together with your spouse, if possible—to show them that the two of you agree about the divorce. Avoid suggesting that the divorce is the "fault" of the other parent.

The discussion should cover these points:

1. You and your spouse intend to end the marriage and live separately. The reason for the separation is that you have

differences that make it impossible to live together peacefully and happily anymore.

2. Although the two of you will stop being husband and wife, you will always be the children's parents. You love them. You always will. That's what parents do.

3. The children will live with one parent, but regularly and frequently stay with the other. Use words like "be with" or "stay with" rather than "visit," which carries the wrong implications. You want the children to keep on loving and being close to both of you.

4. The divorce will be permanent. This is an important point, because initially most children hope they can make their parents get back together again. Explain that even if you and your spouse are cooperating and aren't fighting anymore, it doesn't mean you will get together again. It means that you are being adult. Both of you agree that you'll get along better if you aren't married anymore.

5. The children did not cause the divorce. Even if many of the pre-divorce quarrels were about the children, that's because you and your spouse were having trouble solving your differences, not because the children were bad. Divorce is an adult problem caused by adults.

6. Since they didn't cause it, the children can't fix it. They shouldn't try.

7. You are sorry to cause them pain. You will try to help them get through the rough times, and they will feel better later. Assure them that you'll be there to listen when they want to talk about their bad feelings.

8. Divorce is nothing to be ashamed of. Lots of people get divorced. Mention Aunt Mary and Uncle Joe, or the parents of some of their friends. Because divorce is a private, family matter, you'd prefer they didn't *publicly* discuss the details of the family quarrels they've heard. But it's okay to talk *privately* about their feelings, with friends or teachers, for example. Let them know that it helps sometimes to share and "get things off their chest."

9. Both of you want the children to keep on loving you. Ask them to try not to take sides, even if this may be hard sometimes.

10. Let them know they can come to either of you at any time to talk about problems they're having because of the divorce, so long as they're not just "tattling" on the other parent.

MINIMIZING THE HURT

Once you've decided to split up, you'll have to work to limit the emotional damage to your children. This means cooperating with your spouse even when the two of you are angry with each other.

WHAT TO AVOID

- Fighting in front of the kids
- Blaming your spouse for the divorce
- Threatening to make the kids live with your spouse

WHAT TO AIM FOR

- Preparing the kids for all the changes that will take place.
- Assuring them that they'll be taken care of
- Convincing them the divorce isn't their fault
- Encouraging them not to take sides, but to keep on loving both of their parents
- Helping them express their fear and anger

HOW TO EXPLAIN IT TO THE KIDS

When discussing the divorce with the children, never lie—but don't overwhelm them with truths they aren't old enough to understand.

If there is going to be a trial, or if there are a string of court dates, reassure the kids that it's going to be okay even though Mom or Dad might be temporarily upset. Kids who see a parent agitated and crying sometimes fear more is going on than they're aware of.

Don't go into endless detail about why the marriage broke up.

Don't make promises you aren't sure you can keep. Describe custodial arrangements briefly and matter-of-factly. "You will live with me, but you will see your father every weekend and for Christmas."

Don't say or do anything that will encourage them to "project" too far into the future. Don't allow speculation about what might be necessary if this happens or that happens. For example, don't explain that the custodial agreement involves certain complicated plans for summer vacations and holidays. Explain these when the time comes. If the child asks, "What will we do in the summer?" give a specific answer for the *very next* summer, not for all the summers to come.

Be firm but flexible. Make it clear to the children that the arrangements are definite. Don't allow immediate objections such as, "But I don't want to visit Dad on the Saturdays when I have a baseball game." Indicate that there will be some room to maneuver, and that you will listen to their needs and wishes, but that every weekend is *not* going to involve hours of hassle and negotiation. When you see signs of fear or confusion, ask specific questions: "Is there something about this you don't understand?" "You seem to be bothered by something I just said. Can you tell me what it is?"

Don't show despair, but don't encourage the children in false hopes about reconciliation. Without being harsh, you must make it clear that the divorce is going to take place and that it will be final.

Don't say you have "fallen out of love." They will quickly draw the logical conclusion that if you can stop loving each other, you can stop loving them. Divorce already presents a monumental threat of abandonment to children. Talking about falling out of love can only make it worse.

CHILDREN AND DIVORCE: EMOTIONAL UPHEAVALS

Children automatically blame themselves for their parents' divorce. You cannot repeat too often, by words and by actions, that the children are loved, that they did not cause the divorce, that divorce is something that comes up between two grownups. Say you're sorry it had to happen to them.

As the divorce and recovery process go forward, the children will experience a great many new emotions that you will be seeing in them for the first time. Since children very often do not and cannot talk directly about what they're feeling inside, you will need to be more alert than ever to signs of their distress, and more sensitive to hidden meanings behind their words.

For example, a small child whose parents are divorcing may suddenly develop fears of being kidnapped. Unless there has been a recent kidnapping in the neighborhood, this probably means that the child is afraid of abandonment by his one remaining parent, or terrified that the family might somehow be even further disrupted and torn apart.

Of the many conflicting and frightening feelings the children may undergo, these are the most common:

Guilt: It's my fault. What did I do wrong? How can I hurt this parent by choosing to live with that one?

Hurt and Resentment. Why are they doing this to me? Why can't I have two parents like my friends do? Why did they wait so long before they told me what was going on?

Conflict. I want to see Dad but I don't want to leave Mom. It's better now that they aren't always fighting, but it's sad not being a family. Why does Mom have to cry every time I go to Dad's? Why does Dad want to have that lady there when I visit?

Fear or Panic. If this could happen to me, what else can go wrong? Is my dog going to get run over by a car? I feel sick; am I going to die? Is Mom going to die? or Dad? What will happen to me then?

Loss of Physical Security. What if a robber comes when Dad isn't here? Why do I have to give up my bed and move in with my sister? Why do I have to go to school with the carpool; why can't Mom take me? Why does she have to go to work and leave me with the sitter?

Loss of Continuity and the Stability of Tradition. What are we going to do at Christmas? Why can't we be together the way we always were?

It's wise to remember that children (even more than adults) don't always *know* exactly what their feelings are, or what name to call them. Nor do they know why they are behaving in a certain way. A small child may fly into a tantrum without having any conscious idea why. It takes a wise, sensitive, *alert* parent to identify bad feelings and know what triggered them.

IMPORTANT DON'TS

- Don't use your children to carry your angry messages to your ex-spouse.
- Don't worry your children with "grownup stuff" such as legal or financial problems.
- Don't expect your children to give you emotional support. That's a role for friends, support group members, and/or a therapist.
- Don't make your children feel disloyal for loving both their parents and their stepparents.
- Don't say things like, "Now that Daddy's gone, you're the man of the house." It's unfair to ask your children to fill in like this.

IT HELPS THE CHILDREN WHEN YOU TAKE CARE OF YOURSELF

Children are severely traumatized when they see their parents in open and bitter battle throughout the divorce process. What will most help the kids survive the emotional strain of divorce is seeing their parents cooperate at least on parenting issues, and sensing that even though Mom and Dad have split up, life will still go on.

What will most help you provide emotional stability for your children is doing everything you can to advance your own adjustment and recovery.

Divorce is most damaging to a child when one of her parents is emotionally too overwhelmed to be able to function in everyday life. When this happens, the child faces the added burden of trying to be a parent to her parent.

In one rather dramatic example, a divorced mother who had been wholly dependent on her husband found herself crushed by financial difficulties and the demands of her job, household upkeep, and care of the children. She became so depressed that she was unable to keep up with even simple chores such as doing the dishes. Her children shouldered some of the work and tried to cheer their mother up. At one point, the young teenage daughter was invited to visit a friend in Florida for vacation, but was suddenly stricken by a paralyzing fear of flying.

Fortunately, a relative offered to pay for brief phobia therapy. During one of the first sessions, the girl related a recurring dream in which she was in an airplane, the plane was about to crash, and she kept repeating, "I'm sorry, Mom. I'm sorry, Mom."

To the therapist, the message was simple and clear: The child felt that her mother was helpless without her. Since she was now responsible for her mother, she dared not fly; if the plane crashed, her mother would be left alone and helpless. This also reflected the child's hidden fears of abandonment.

In this case, it was obvious that the mother needed professional help more than the child.

Throughout divorce, then, it's the parents' job to handle their own feelings and behavior so that their children will have a clear example of responsible adult behavior. Boys and girls need to see their father behaving in ways that are both strong and sensitive; they need to know that he is capable of feeling sad and hurt, but that he can cope with it. They need to see a mother who has her own inner strength and resources, and a strong sense of identity that's independent of marriage and a husband. They need both parents to show them a model of adult cooperation, resolution of conflicts, and acceptance of the responsibilities that they voluntarily chose—first in marrying, then in having children, and finally in determining on divorce as the only solution to a problem.

What if you're not up to all this lofty idealism? What if your ex-spouse is someone you loathe and wish you never had to see or talk to again? What if you feel you can't cooperate on parenting issues? The answer is: For the sake of the children, who deeply need both of their parents, you have to **try**.

Of course, if you're seething with anger at your ex-spouse, that's something you'll need to acknowledge to your children; they will know it anyway, and they'll be confused and disoriented if you pretend it isn't so. But having acknowledged your anger, you can still do your utmost to stay calm and businesslike when dealing with difficult co-parenting issues.

It's far from easy, but the results are well worth the effort. The children will notice and appreciate your self-control. They'll learn from you, by example, an extremely valuable lesson: that a grownup can set personal feelings aside long enough to take care of business. And as you gain confidence that you can indeed manage your anger, you'll feel better about yourself—more mature, more competent, wiser.

So even if you feel like tearing your hair out every time you and your ex-spouse disagree over plans for the children, don't let your anger destroy you. Distance yourself from that anger, retrench, and keep thinking and negotiating.

If you can do it yourself, that's great. However, this is also a time to reflect and get feedback from others. You may decide to go for individual therapy. Or you may find a group setting that feels right: a Divorce Anonymous group, for instance, or some other divorce recovery program. (Fortunately, there's a nation-wide move to offer help to people struggling through divorce. As this book went to press, in fact, Alvarado Parkway Institute was initiating a special divorce recovery track.) If there's a history of abuse, you may also want to get legal help. By all means do so—if it's genuinely in the children's best interest.

With the passage of time, you will become more and more expert at distinguishing between your own emotional needs and those of your children—a skill that will eventually make you a better, stronger parent. This is a process that requires courage and persistence, so have faith in yourself and stick with it. It won't be easy, but you can do it. You don't have to do it alone, either, so why try to be a hero? Give yourself a break, and go for the support you deserve.

EMOTIONAL SUPPORT FOR KIDS

According to psychologists, these situations encourage the "best" (that is, least damaging) outcome for children of divorce:

Absence of Open Conflict. There should be no verbal or physical attacks on each other, no "divorce disagreements" in front of the children. Parents should communicate and be cooperative with each other.

A Good Relationship with Each Parent Individually. Parents need to act like parents—to set limits and uphold values, while at the same time being affectionate and caring. In the typical situation where the father is the noncustodial parent, he should continue to be a father, not a sort of uncle or pal who merely entertains the children on weekends. Their visits to him should not be an endless round of trips to the circus, but should approximate normal family life. A father could involve the children in some home project such as building a table, fixing up his new apartment, or just washing the car.

Continued and Uninterrupted Evidence of Love and Care by Both Parents. More than ever, you'll have to make sure the kids feel your support and concern. If you and your spouse will share custody of the children, both of you must be on your toes. While the marriage was still intact, one of you may have taken care of most of the children's physical and emotional needs. Now that you're splitting up, both of you will need to fill that role. A newly single father will soon learn that changing bedsheets, doing loads of laundry, and driving kids to their friends' houses are ways of showing love.

Organization and Planning. Children need structure but not rigidity. Things should happen on time. Promises should be kept, boundaries observed. Parents should listen to the children's requests for changes in visiting times or sleeping arrangements, but should keep any changes within reasonable limits to avoid chaos and insecurity. Children's needs should be respected, but the kids should not be allowed always to have their own way or "rule the roost" because of the parents' guilt over subjecting them to the divorce.

The Availability of Other Support. This could be grandparents, other close relatives, guidance counselors, friends, or teachers. When each parent begins to build up a circle of new friends, this helps to combat the children's sense of isolation from the community. Seek professional help promptly if the children begin to show signs of depression, isolation from friends, major changes in appetite, alterations in personality not related to normal development, or difficulties in school.

Encouragement by Parents of Individuality, Self-Sufficiency, and Mature Decision-Making. Children should be allowed to make decisions for themselves when appropriate, but not forced to make decisions beyond their years or capacity. They should be encouraged to accept family duties and responsibilities, and to contribute to family plans, but they shouldn't be burdened with responsibilities that are rightfully the parents'.

CHILDREN'S NEEDS AT DIFFERENT AGES

Divorce affects children differently depending on their age at the time the marriage breaks up.

Preschoolers need the reassurance of frequent contact with both parents. Even brief periods of contact are better than nothing. Young children need caring people to hold, feed, bathe, talk to, and play with them.

Schoolchildren need longer periods of contact with both parents, including sleeping at both parents' houses. They need to feel they're allowed to love their parents, stepparents, and all the people who are good to them. They need both of their parents to be involved with their teachers and their schoolwork.

Teenagers need ongoing contact with both parents, but some freedom and flexibility to make personal decisions. They need privacy, frequent contact with their peers, guidance about behavior (from both parents), and freedom from having to take sides in the divorce.

COMMUNICATION

Central to all these issues of divorce recovery, for both parents and children, is the matter of communication between the parents.

After the divorce becomes final, parents enter a different and in many ways more difficult period. They are still parents, but they're no longer parents together. Although they are no longer a couple, there remains an urgent need for them to continue communicating and relating as parents—to "coparent," as psychologists would say. Studies have shown that some 85 percent of divorced parents continue to maintain some kind of direct contact with each other for at least a year after the breakup. In one study, two-thirds of the parents talked with each other on the phone at least once a month, one third at least once a week. About two-thirds of the parents also had direct contact, and discussed child-care issues in person, with some regularity—usually when the father picked up the children or brought them home. About a third of parents had specifically arranged times to talk about issues involving the children, either in person or on the phone. About one-fourth to one-third spent time together with the children as a family, most often for special occasions such as birthdays or school events. Some even continued to share major holidays such as Thanksgiving.

But at least half of the parents in this particular study found these contacts difficult, and often found themselves in conflict when they discussed the children. Not surprisingly, money was the most common area of conflict. Another sore point was how the children were reacting and adjusting to the divorce.

It isn't easy to continue filling the demanding role of "parent" in coordination with someone from whom you've just broken off your most fundamental relationship. There are, of course, amicable and civilized divorces, followed by healthy and relatively smooth readjustments of parental roles. But for a great majority of divorced couples, this is not the case. Continuing as coparents can be a difficult or even overwhelming adjustment, especially if the breaking-off was angry and ugly. How can you cooperate with someone whose every quirk or attitude gets under your skin, or whose very existence overwhelms you with sorrow or rage?

COPARENTING

Perhaps the most essential step is to start looking at your ex-spouse not as your ex-spouse, but as the other parent of your children. This will require a prodigious effort of awareness and objectivity, but—given time—it can be done. You may simply try to see that person as your children do—leaving yourself out of the picture as much as possible. You may try to think of your relationship with your ex-partner as something completely new—a kind of business arrangement, with the children as the business and the two of you as the executives. Most of all, you should look into your own feelings and see how they are intruding into the coparenting relationship. Coparent cooperation is difficult in the face of power struggles, grudge-bearing, and urges for revenge.

It's not necessary to be right—especially when you're wrong! If you and your ex-partner continue your struggle for the upper hand into your coparenting relationship, neither of you will ever win, the children will definitely lose, and you'll seriously jeopardize your recovery. Divorced couples who have no children have an easier time getting on with the job of recovering and rebuilding their own lives, because the ex-spouse isn't *there* in the background to rekindle angers and stir up old feelings. However, coparents *can* prevent this rekindling if they work at it. The way to begin is to close the door on the old relationship, especially the part of it that involves emotional control over each other.

First, try to let go of the other person. Keep telling yourself that this person, who is no longer the most important person in your life, has no power to make you happy or unhappy, no power to make you feel good or bad about yourself. This is one of the most important issues for your *own* recovery, but until it is resolved you must not let it interfere with the work of parenting. It may be difficult to separate these issues, but it's crucial that you try.

Therefore, when confronting your ex-partner over parenting issues, keep these things in mind:

- Every time you focus on your ex-partner's behavior, get irritated at him, criticize him, or blame him, you're letting him control your feelings and thoughts. You're wasting energy refighting old emotional battles, rather than concentrating on what should be the real issue: the children.

- You may feel angry at your ex-partner. This is a natural postdivorce feelings. But you need to resolve this anger yourself, and remember that the anger *really has nothing to do with the children*. You may think you are angry because your ex-partner is doing this or that in regard to the children, but the more probable cause is your basic anger over the divorce. Try to examine the immediate trigger of your anger and separate it from discussions of child care. Although it's important to express anger and work through it, parenting discussions are not the time or place for this. When you find yourself angry and ready to strike back, the first thing to do is *shut up*. Think before you speak. Ask yourself if this is really a fight over the children, or if it's something else. Consider what response is going to serve the children best. Then reply.

- Don't get obsessed with resentment over the way your ex-partner used to treat you. Don't keep going over past slights and insults while you're trying to deal with parenting issues. They will occupy space in your mind that should be devoted to the welfare of the children. In addition, it's unhealthy for you. Your resentment hurts you more than it hurts your ex-partner; you're the one who's being eaten up by this acid.

- Keep in mind that regardless of marital conflicts, your ex-partner has rights and *needs* as a parent which must be respected for the children's sake.

- Trying to "punish" your ex-partner through the children will only punish the children, and leave you with an unnecessary burden of guilt.

- Keep your side of the street clean. What your ex-partner does on his or her side of the street is not your problem. The better you do your job, the better your ex-partner is likely to do.

- It's important that you come away from meetings with your ex-partner *feeling good about yourself*, feeling that you have done your best for the children. Your ex-partner's opinions about you don't matter any more; they don't make you what you are. What matters is your opinion about how well you're looking after your children's interests—which definitely includes fostering, and not defeating, their good relationship with their other parent. When you compromise or avoid a fight in order to be a good parent, you aren't giving in or abdicating your "right to be right."

- When you and your ex-partner are dealing with parental issues, always keep your behavior or conversations centered on the children. Leave the marriage out of it. The marriage was *then;* taking care of the children is *now*.

What's essential to remember is that the more conflict there is over the children—the more you let the anger, resentment and bitterness of the divorce get in the way of dealing with parenting—the longer the children will suffer and the longer *you* will suffer. A certain amount of pain is inevitable, but the truth is that you have a great deal of control over how long you suffer from it.

Nevertheless, there are limits. If all your efforts at cooperation and accommodation yield nothing but hostility and a persistent refusal to meet you halfway, or if you have real and substantial reasons for believing that your ex-partner is treating your children in a way that will harm them, and if your belief is confirmed by another objective observer, you have a right and an obligation to protect your children by legal means.

EMOTIONAL TASKS FOR KIDS

Like parents, children have specific emotional "tasks" to work through during and after a divorce. Your attitude and behavior can do much to help them with this work. Judith Wallerstein, author of *Surviving the Breakup* and *Second Chances* and director of a historic ten-year study of divorced families, summed up these tasks as follows:

1. **Understanding the Divorce.** In the beginning, this means learning to accept the reality of the divorce, and separating it from fantasies about reconciliation or fears of further loss. Later (and with older children) it means understanding how the divorce came about, and learning positive lessons from seeing how the postdivorce problems were solved.

2. **Strategic Withdrawal.** Children need to get on with their own lives, resume their normal activities and friendships, grow up, and gain independence. They need to be encouraged to move the divorce out of the center of their concerns and refocus on their own tasks. For small children, this means that they should be encouraged to be *children,* and not carry adult responsibility in the emotional aftermath of divorce. For adolescents, it means being encouraged to go through the normal adolescent process of moving from a family-centered to a peer-centered life.

3. **Dealing with Loss.** In divorce, children lose a cohesive family and partly (or completely) lose a parent, too. This is the most difficult aspect of divorce for children. It makes them feel

powerless, rejected, unloved, and unloveable. Children can learn to overcome their feeling that the divorce was their fault, that the parent who left didn't love them enough to stay, that if only they were better they could get their parents back together. But this takes time, and most of all it takes two major contributions from the parents: first, a mature coparenting relationship that includes functional arrangements for children's stays with the absent parent; second, a good, close relationship with the parent who doesn't have custody.

4. Dealing with Anger. Children get angry at their parents for making them unhappy. To them, divorce signifies that their parents didn't care enough about them to stay together and continue to do their jobs as parents. It seems selfish and irresponsible. Anger is fueled by their fear at seeing their parents unhappy, disorganized, and coping badly. In time and with appropriate help, children can recognize their parents not just as parents, but as adults who have their own needs and emotions. They can learn to forgive parents for their ordinary human mistakes. This will be more likely to happen, and sooner, if the parents continue to express their love and concern for the children, act as responsible (if separate) parents, and go about their own job of recovery as rapidly and efficiently as possible—while understanding, accepting, and forgiving their children's anger toward them.

5. Working out Guilt. Children may feel guilty in several ways: fearing that they caused the divorce, assuming that by living with one parent they are rejecting the other, and even thinking that they have no right to get over the divorce, be happy, and get on with their own lives if their parents are still suffering. The same parental attitudes mentioned in the previous paragraph can be helpful here.

6. Accepting the Permanence of the Divorce. Fantasies of reconciliation may be a necessary way of protecting a child's fragile emotions against too large a dose of reality. But bit by bit children need to let go of this form of denial. It can take a long time; some children still refuse to accept the reality of divorce as much as five or ten years later. It requires patience and understanding from the parents, and a hefty dose of time and growing up.

7. Taking a Chance on Love. Children of divorce are handicapped by the deep inner knowledge that love may not last, that commitment to another person can bring loss and pain. Some children of divorce suffer from this burden of fear throughout life. Divorced parents need a tremendous amount of commitment to support their children's growth, encourage them to take risks, and help them accept this reality: that life holds no guarantees, but that holding back for want of guarantees means living life less than fully.

PAIN, THEN GAIN, FOR KIDS TOO

It also helps to remember that recovery brings its rewards to your children as well as yourself. With your help, children can extract from the divorce experience lessons that will be valuable to them throughout life. For example:

- Change is not necessarily bad. It's better to make changes than to keep living in misery.
- Life brings disappointments, but people can survive them and learn from them.
- You can minimize pain and disappointment if you're flexible, learn some coping skills, and use them appropriately.
- We are all powerless over certain life events, but we are *not* powerless to deal with them, survive them, and use them for learning and growth.
- Everything is easier if you ask for help, and if you and those you care for work together.

Agency or school-based support groups for children, adolescents and adults involved in divorce have been established in many areas. Some emphasize cognitive mastery of the divorce experience. Others permit or encourage expression of suppressed feelings. Still others advocate a quick return to customary activities, plus a building of friendship groups. There's persuasive evidence that these groups do provide comfort and can alleviate loneliness.

Many people assume that if the parents get help or join a support group, there will be a "trickle down" benefit to the children, but the scientific evidence does *not* confirm this. When parents feel better, their parenting may get better, but there's no guarantee that the child will feel better. In fact, for this reason, Divorce Anonymous plans to establish support groups for children of divorce.

Asking for help with divorce is even more crucial for couples with children than for childless couples. Social supports tend to fall away from a divorcing family, at least temporarily, while friends and extended families rearrange themselves and come to terms with the new alignments. This may exaggerate the children's already severe sense of loneliness and isolation.

SOURCES OF COUNSELING SERVICES FOR DIVORCING PARENTS:

- American Association for Marriage and Family Therapists
  1717 K Street, N.W.
  Washington, DC 20036
- Conciliation Court or Family Court
- Family service agencies
- Mental health agencies
- Child guidance clinics
- Private mental health professionals
- Family doctors
- Ministers, priests, rabbis

DO YOU NEED PROFESSIONAL HELP?*

Some divorces are particularly difficult on parents and children. If breaking up is making it impossible for your family to function, you should consider getting professional counseling. The Association of Family and Conciliation Courts suggests seeking professional help in any of the following cases:

1. You and your spouse are unable to communicate with each other
2. There is violence between any members of your family
3. Someone in the family has ongoing anxiety or depression
4. Someone in the family has an alcohol or drug problem
5. People in your family are unable to talk about their feelings

---

*From "Twenty Questions Divorcing Parents Ask About Their Children," a pamphlet published by the Association of Family and Conciliation Courts, 329 West Wilson Street, Madison, WI 53703 (608) 251-4001.

6. Your spouse is totally uninvolved with your child
7. Your spouse, or your child, shows delinquent or self-destructive behavior
8. Your child withdraws from normal everyday contact with other people
9. Your child is having problems at school
10. Your child is taking sides against either you or your spouse.

Remember, there are many different sources for counseling and therapy. Choose a therapist just as carefully as you would a family doctor or a lawyer. It's appropriate to ask about the therapist's credentials, special training, and experience. And even if you're plagued by financial worries, don't assume you can't afford professional help; some therapists base their charges on the client's ability to pay.

7

꧁꧂꧁꧂꧁꧂꧁꧂꧁꧂꧁꧂꧁꧂꧁꧂

Time Heals All (If You Help It)

*"All earthly pain is due to our inability to release that which must
be set free."*

—Anonymous

The healing power of time is not a myth but a reality. Given
enough time, most emotional pain eases and eventually disappears altogether. This does not mean that emotional pain has no
lasting effect. Some people are damaged by it; some remain at a
standstill. Others grow and mature—but this isn't something
that happens all by itself. If you want to grow through your
pain, you will need to give time a hand. Yes, you can help time
do its healing work, and in more ways than one. That's what this
chapter will be about.

First, let's acknowledge that the effects of passing time vary
depending on the nature of the emotional pain. After the death
of a loved one, for example, the pain of grief usually yields to
the healing process of healthy mourning, although this may take
from months to years. Divorce is a somewhat different situation.
When you lose a spouse through natural death, the mourning
process is free from the unresolved anger, guilt, and sense of
failure that typically affect you during and after divorce. (Be-
reaved people often do feel anger, but this is an anger against
fate or the unfairness of death. In divorce, your anger focuses on
your spouse's shortcomings, or against yourself for real or
imagined failures that you believe contributed to the breakup of
the marriage. The former anger is "cleaner" and yields more
easily to the softening effect of time.)

Furthermore, time alone does not necessarily heal, especially after the more complicated losses involved in divorce. In the face of a determined (if unacknowledged) effort to hang on to pain—or to old, ineffective ways of dealing with it, such as denial, self-pity, blame-shifting, resentment, or an obsession with vengeance—time is powerless to heal.

Along with all the other emotions and practical burdens, divorce causes a great deal of confusion and mixed feelings. It's practically impossible to sort these all out when you are in the midst of them, or even to believe that eventually things will become more clear and less painful. In the acute stage of divorce, you need to concentrate on practical problems, and to confront and understand only your most immediate, powerful, and crippling emotions.

Only when the final break has occurred, the papers are signed, the children's future is arranged, and you have the privacy and breathing room to take stock, can you begin to deal with the longer-term problems of divorce. (If you have practiced preventive medicine and benefitted from good counseling and support during the acute phase, this will be much easier.)

HOW LONG DOES RECOVERY TAKE?

Most people want to know how long it will take to recover from their divorce. There is no ready answer. Experts have a variety of formulas: one month for every year of marriage; one year for every five years of marriage, and so on. In reality, recovery from divorce is a lot like recovery from any physical illness. There is probably an irreducible minimum of time required (say, three days after a particular surgical operation before you can leave the hospital), but beyond that it's a highly individual matter. Some people bounce back quickly from illness or surgery; others recover slowly, bit by bit. So the accurate, if emotionally unsatisfactory, answer is, "It takes as long as it takes."

It is important to remember this if you begin to feel you'll never get over it; if you perceive that other people are "doing just fine" after a divorce while you are still suffering from headaches, insomnia, and depression. As long as you're making a conscious effort to recover, getting help through therapy or group support, and energetically seeking self-understanding, then you can relax a little in the knowledge that you are doing all you can and that time will do the rest.

EVERYTHING DEPENDS ON YOUR SITUATION

The long-term problems of divorce can vary enormously. From the divorced woman who has been physically abused and is terrified that her ex-husband is still going to "come after her," to the man who feels the divorce settlement "robbed him blind," to the couple whose marriage fell apart through boredom and whose feelings for each other are now no stronger than indifference—different divorces raise different recovery issues.

Common factors that affect recovery are:

- **Your Life Stage at the Time of Divorce.** Two young people who married right out of high school, and divorced after a few years, will probably have a quicker adjustment than the couple who have spent much of their adult lives together, raised children, and shared a long history of partnership, family, and friends.

- **Whether the Marriage was "Comfortable" or "Passionate."** Marriages based solely on intense sexual attraction tend to break up more readily, and more stormily, than those based partly on shared social backgrounds and economic considerations.

- **Money Matters.** How easy or difficult it will be to support separate households will have an important influence on recovery. The more you have to worry about money, the less energy you have for emotional healing. Divorces involving either a great deal of money and property, or so little money that post-divorce survival for one partner will be difficult, pose special problems and greater obstacles to eventual recovery.

- **Support.** Continued close relationships with family and friends who are understanding, patient, and encouraging provide stability and make it much easier to recover. Divorce is very hard on people who are isolated, who had become a part of the spouse's extended family and thus lose that family through divorce, or who had few friends before the divorce and lost most of them afterward. Counseling can help anyone who is divorcing, but is especially vital for those who lack other support systems.

- **Expectations and Fantasy.** In this tail end of the twentieth century, our society has been transformed by new sexual freedoms, the altered status of women, and the wide prevalence of divorce. Nevertheless, most Americans still grow up with a highly romantic and optimistic view of marriage. Eternal love and happiness, high-achieving children, a house in the suburbs, and a two-car garage are assumed to be the natural outcome of the marriage vows. Even though "no-fault" divorce has become a legal reality, most people still think of divorce as a personal and social failure.

The higher the expectations, the greater the disappointment. If a marital breakup is assumed to represent a derailing of some natural process, or a symptom of some serious flaw in the character of one or both partners, the result will be bitterness, self-blame, and regret.

CHANCES FOR "SUCCESSFUL" RECOVERY

Unrealistic expectations and fantasies about life after divorce are common. Since the 1970s, there has risen a popular notion that divorce will lead to a gloriously free new life filled with excitement, adventures, glamour, romance, and enhanced career opportunities. Hopes are high that the "second chance" will be better than the first. Dealing with reality—which may or may not be immensely satisfying and enriching—is the biggest challenge and greatest opportunity of the long-term recovery process.

Statistically, the odds seem unfavorable. But statistics deal with large populations; they don't accurately describe any individual. Statistically, the odds against winning a $20 million lottery are astronomical, but *somebody* always wins it.

Statistically, then, divorced people suffer higher than average rates of alcoholism, depression, other psychiatric disorders, physical illness, hospitalization, and suicide. (However, people who divorce may be ill or troubled. For many, the problems just mentioned are triggers, not results, of divorce. "Pre-existing conditions" will be discussed later in this chapter.)

Even people who escape these dramatic after-effects of divorce are not exempt from difficulties. Almost twenty years ago a well-known divorce counselor, Judith Wallerstein, founder and executive director of the Center for the Family in Transition in California, conducted a study of sixty families undergoing divorce. Ten years later she re-studied these families; this was the first known investigation of the long-term effects of divorce on different family members. Even though she had extensive experience in divorce practice, Wallerstein was surprised to discover how common it was for serious problems to persist even after such a long post-divorce period. Her study demonstrated vividly that divorce is not something that you go through and then just "get over."

Wallerstein found that 80 percent of the women and 50 percent of the men "affirmed" the divorce decision; that is, they thought it had been the best thing to do. Their reactions generally confirmed that divorce does "undo" the mistakes of the marriage and bring relief from strife. But life wasn't always better after divorce. Reasons included poverty for divorced women, loneliness and disorganization for divorced men, and lasting emotional trauma for children whose parents had divorced.

Also, in many cases, unrealistic expectations about life after divorce exaggerated people's disappointment, dismay, and bitterness.

Don't expect divorce to produce immediate benefits other than *relief*—relief from quarreling, and from the daily anxieties of sharing a life with someone you once loved but toward whom you now feel indifference, animosity, or even hatred. You can look forward to the possibility of many benefits, but you cannot *begin* recovery in a blissful state of joy and fulfillment. Maybe your divorce will turn out to be "the best thing that could have happened," but you haven't reached that stage yet. You can't start from the final outcome. You can only start from where you are—from the understanding that divorce is a *process*, that it hurts a lot, and that if you move through it at your own pace with resiliency and courage, there is a definite opportunity for a transformed life.

LOOKING INWARD

One of the first and most difficult jobs of long-term recovery is confronting your inner self. Most people are afraid of self-knowledge. Members of 12-step recovery groups, for example, almost always find the fourth step the hardest to take. This step entails making "a searching and fearless moral inventory" of yourself. It requires that you examine your life without excuses, rationalization, blame-shifting, or self-deception. The idea is to *take responsibility;* that is, recognize and accept whatever acts you have done that caused harm to yourself or someone else. However, the idea is also to pay attention to your positive qualities and understand that your shortcomings are only human. Make an effort to overcome your negative characteristics, but don't let them fill you with shame. The fourth step says, in effect: know yourself, forgive yourself, change yourself.

This excellent recipe for recovering from divorce may be easier to follow with guidance or counseling. One of the "good" things about divorce is this: it involves such massive change that you're apt to decide, "Since so many other things are changing, now is a good time to change myself."

Change leads to self-knowledge, and self-knowledge encourages further change. It's a good idea to seek competent help in adapting to this cycle. Divorce involves so much conflict about identity, the meaning of the past, the pressures of the present, and the uncertainty of the future that you may not know where to start. But whatever you decide, trust yourself. Know that you have deeply buried reserves of strength and energy, and make up your mind to keep experimenting until you tap into those reserves. Whether you call this hidden strength God, or the ultimate being, or simply a "higher power," remember that it's there, and make a habit of invoking its power. This is your key to focusing on the here-and-now, releasing yourself from crippling anxieties, and getting on with the process of recovery.

TAKING STOCK

Whether or not you've decided on a counselor or therapist, you can take stock of your present situation by trying to identify what bothers you the most. These are some of the issues that cause people the most trouble during divorce:

- **Identity.** Often it's the woman who has an identity problem, especially if her husband initiated the divorce. Feelings of unworthiness can seriously undermine her self-esteem. If her husband was her primary source of identity, she is likely to feel not only abandoned but personally "lost." Someone in this position wonders where she should begin. It can help if she puts some structure into her life while searching for a new identity. A job, volunteer work (in particular, involvement in her community), making new friends and new connections that are specifically *her own* rather than leftovers from the marriage—all are significant practical steps. Another ego booster is to take *positive* stock: she should write down a list of assets, strengths, and personal qualities (those that are completely unrelated to marriage and husband), recognize their value, and start to build on them.

■ **Excessive Self-Criticism.** Although self-knowledge is an important goal, it's crucial to make sure that your self-knowledge is accurate and not distorted by self-loathing. Some divorced people blame everything on the ex-spouse and nourish their hatred of this person, for years or even decades. But people who are fundamentally self-critical are likely to fall into the opposite trap, obsessively asking themselves, "What did I do wrong? How could I have prevented this divorce? Why did I mess up so badly? It was all my fault."

■ **Selfishness Versus Self-Support and Self-Respect.** It's important to distinguish between these. The first implies feeling and doing things in a self-centered way, regardless of what your actions may impose on or take away from others. The second suggests a healthy interest in your own well-being alongside concern and respect for others.

Can you distinguish between your "wants" and your "needs"? If you're a woman, chances are you can't. In our society, most women have grown up in a tradition of nurturing, sacrifice, and service to spouse and family. Other people's needs come first. As a result, few women, especially married women who routinely take care of their family, know how to recognize and satisfy their own needs. Divorced women who have this problem need to accept that it's right and good to care for themselves. When a woman takes care of herself *first*, it strengthens her. Then she's able to give of herself to her family without losing sight of who she is.

In our work with women's therapy groups, we have found that it's a wonderful revelation to women when they discover that they can see and fulfill their own emotional needs. Self-discovery can be exciting and fun. You can start simply, making a list of those things that you always wanted to do, but never did because of the demands of taking care of your family. For example:

- Going back to school, or just taking a course in something that interests you.
- Making specific plans for free time or rest.
- Learning to enjoy your own company.
- Starting a new project, or developing a new skill.
- Making friends with other women—not couples, men, or people who were in any way concerned with you when you were married.
- Joining an organization—political, environmental, or other.

- **Communication.** In some ways, believe it or not, men are psychologically much more vulnerable than women. Most men don't really have close male friends. They relate to each other in the business world or through sports, but they aren't intimate with men in a way that allows them to talk about deep personal feelings and needs. As a result, men are likely to prematurely and precipitately seek out a female companion in the immediate post-divorce period. Often what they are looking for is not sex, love, or a housekeeper, but merely *someone to talk to*.

  Both men and women need a listener, a sounding board—not necessarily someone who gives advice, but someone who willingly lends an understanding ear. Feelings that are bottled up, unexpressed, will eventually either fester or explode.

- **Unresolved Issues.** At some point, you should turn your focus away from the divorce as the central emotional issue, and begin to deal with psychological issues unrelated to your marriage: childhood pain or deprivation, abuse, abandonment, low self-esteem, or perhaps self-destructive behavior such as eating disorders, alcoholism, or drug abuse. If not clarified and resolved, these issues will continue to cloud the atmosphere of your life after divorce.

  Addictions, which are among the most serious of these problems, deserve number one priority when you're aiming for long-term recovery. Alcohol abuse, drug abuse, or an eating disorder may have predated the divorce, or developed during or after divorce. Either way, recovery from an addiction can bring unexpected rewards. People who successfully overcome an addiction, through a combination of therapy and a 12-step recovery program, find that they also resolve many of the problems stemming from their divorce and even from certain childhood traumas.

Divorce, however, poses special risks for people with addictions. Under the strain of a deteriorating marriage, an addiction may get much worse. If you were already recovering from an addiction, the shock and stress of divorce presents a major threat of relapse.

■ **Hidden Motivations.** What makes you do the things you do? The post-divorce period is a time for solving present problems and building for the future. But if you're not careful, you may start to flounder among influences left over from your marriage. You may unwittingly practice a kind of self-punishment, denying yourself the opportunities your new freedom offers. You may automatically isolate yourself, avoid new activities, drown yourself in overwork, or lose yourself in excessive devotion to your children.

A divorced person sometimes perpetuates personal suffering in an attempt to "get even" with the ex-spouse. It's as if the person is saying to the former mate, "I'll show you how much you made me suffer. I'll keep on suffering, and you'll see how much I'm suffering, and then you'll be sorry." This kind of guilt-tripping usually backfires. The ex-spouse recognizes it as childish behavior, resents it, and does everything possible to ignore it.

As we mentioned, previously, newly divorced men are apt to mimic what they think is appropriate "singles" behavior—for instance, practically living in singles' bars—for lack of any better idea of what to do with their time. They're likely to put on a good show of "doing much better" than they did while married, by dating constantly, taking glamorous vacations, making luxurious or frivolous purchases (a motorcycle, a boat, etc.)—as if to say, "See, I don't need you in order to be happy," and "See what you kept me from having while we were married." This behavior is dangerous, especially if it becomes habitual instead of giving way to more honest and self-fulfilling activities. Self-assessment and self-knowledge involve examining your motives, asking yourself, "What am I doing with my life, and what is it leading to?'"

RECOVERY STEP-BY-STEP

Throughout the work of long-term recovery from divorce, it's important to keep in mind that there are stages to recovery. The severity of the stages, and the amount of time they consume, can vary enormously, but nearly everyone goes through all the stages. Knowing this can help you accept that your unpleasant feelings are not necessarily unhealthy or "sick," but may be normal and even essential. The stages of recovery from divorce closely resemble some of the classic stages of mourning, with certain differences:

1. Denial. Pretending that "This isn't really happening to me" is self-protective up to a point, but of course it postpones the inevitable moment of dealing with reality. It's the noninitiator of the divorce who's likely to experience severe denial.

2. Anger. Usually anger develops next, breaking down and replacing the denial. Anger stems from multiple sources: feelings of betrayal, money problems, new and frightening choices, misunderstanding by family and friends, disappointed expectations, jealousy, or self-blame. It's important to get help with understanding how much of your anger is justified, and how much is simply childish self-indulgence.

3. Bargaining. You may try to bargain with your partner to get what you want: reconciliation, a chance to try again, a chance to apologize and "make up for what you did wrong." In addition, you may bargain with your own feelings, allowing yourself to dwell endlessly on "what ifs": What if I lost weight and styled my hair differently? What if I hadn't squandered all that money on the stock market? What if we hadn't had children? What if we *had* had children?

These mind games originate from guilt, fear of the unknown, attempts to postpone the inevitable, or other mixed emotions associated with divorce. The divorce initiator may have gone through the bargaining stage in anticipation of the divorce, but may have to live through it again once the splitup gets under way. The noninitiator is more likely to bargain actively, seeking reconciliation or a second chance, and it's even possible that a trial reconciliation will result. In rare cases, two people who divorce each other actually get remarried. But the emotional realities of divorce make this highly unlikely for most couples.

4. Depression. Some people are depressed during the divorce process itself, some right after the divorce becomes final, and some much later—just when they thought they were getting over the divorce. Symptoms of depression include changes in appetite, sleep irregularities, poor concentration, inability to make decisions, low self-esteem, a sense of failure, self-anger, and sometimes suicidal thoughts. With time and emotional support, your divorce-linked depression may abate. If it doesn't, it needs to be diagnosed and treated.

5. Acceptance. The healing process is not a straight line, but a series of ups and downs. Although the general trend is positive, it's often a case of two steps forward and one step back. By working through the stages of divorce one after another, you'll eventually reach the final stage. At this point you'll be looking forward more often than you look back. You'll enjoy the pleasures of freedom, a new self-identity, and the many opportunities of a new life. You will accept the divorce as real and final. You'll recognize more clearly what went wrong with the marriage, and why you weren't necessarily to blame for it. Perhaps you'll even come to understand, and forgive, both yourself and your ex-spouse.

GOALS OF RECOVERY

In recovery from divorce, the most important goal is emotional balance and self-sufficiency—knowing how to rely on your own inner resources and develop your own personal strengths, rather than depending on your marriage or your partner. A crucial step toward this goal is what therapists call "closure" or "psychic divorce."

These terms simply mean that, emotionally, both the marriage and the divorce are *really over*.

Although the expression "good divorce" may seem like a contradiction in terms, the outcome of some divorces may indeed be considered "good." In these cases, a key factor is closure.

Several years ago, two divorce specialists—Kenneth Kressler of Rutgers University and Morton Deutsch of Columbia University—asked marital therapy specialists who had considerable experience in divorce work what they considered the characteristics of a "good divorce."

The experts agreed on several essential points. A good (or constructive) divorce, they said, shows the following features:*

The Ex-Spouses Act Genuinely Civil Toward Each Other. Even the noninitiator comes to accept that divorce is the best solution to their problems. Negotiations over practical matters don't degenerate into futile shouting matches, and disagreements don't lead to a total breakdown of communication. Each partner leaves the marriage with a balanced view of the divorce and of each other. As one expert said, "The good outcome to me is where the individual, without either self-blame or blaming the other, has been able to look at the marriage and say in retrospect, "Here were the good things, which were nice, and they are part of me; here are the things that went wrong, for these and these reasons."

In a good divorce, looking back is an occasional activity, not an obsession. Regrets are real, but not crushing. The ex-partners are able to cooperate on practical matters such as parenting. They have a relatively objective view of each other.

There's an old saying, "All widows were married to saints; all divorced women were married to devils." In the good divorce, the ex-partner is neither saint nor devil, but someone you once loved and now love no longer. He or she is someone who—like you—has faults and assets and all the other qualities that make people human.

In the good divorce, when it's settled, it's settled. Conflicts, especially in court, do not stretch out over years. Hatreds get thrown out with all the other debris of the past.

Emotional Damage to the Children is Kept to a Minimum. No child escapes divorce unharmed. But in a constructive divorce, the couple try to think and behave as *parents,* not as a husband and wife who are at war with each other. Emotional and legal skirmishes are kept within bounds, and are not played out in front of the children. Parents do not attack each other; one parent doesn't try to "poison the children's minds" against the other one. Both parents recognize—and act upon—the children's need for two parents, even if one parent is only part-time. In the kindest but firmest way, parents try to help

---

*Kressel, Kenneth, *The Process of Divorce: How Professionals and Couples Negotiate Settlements.* New York: Basic Books, Inc., 1985, pp. 66–81.

their children accept the finality of the divorce and give up their fantasies of living together as a family again. In a good divorce, parents do all they can to provide their children with good examples of reasonable and caring adult behavior. They also do everything they can to help the children overcome the trauma of divorce, deal with their emotional pain, and grow from it.

The Divorced Individual Undergoes Personal Growth. Feelings of failure and self-blame are discarded as the person gains self-knowledge, self-reliance, an ability to cope, a sense of personal value, and the ability to form satisfying new relationships. With this increased maturity, the divorced person either lives a rich and productive single life, or forms a lasting new attachment that's free of the neurotic or immature characteristics of the first marriage.

ONE WOMAN'S CLOSURE

Rosalie's story is a good example of a "closure" experience. Three years after her divorce, Rosalie was still torn apart by emotional conflict. She felt like a failure, wasn't able to form satisfactory new relationships, and came away from her therapy sessions feeling she wasn't making any progress. When her therapist eventually told her that her problem was lack of closure, Rosalie suddenly clicked into action. She sat down and made a list of points to discuss and questions to ask. Then she got together with her ex-husband for coffee. Afterward she told her therapist:

"I am so pleased and relieved. We admitted that neither of us was perfect. Simon acknowledged that we'd had some good times, that I wasn't a horrible person. Just hearing him tell me I wasn't a horrible person made me feel okay. At the end of the meeting I wished him well and he wished me well. We hugged each other. And if we bump into each other again, well, it won't be so bad."

8

⌐⌐⌐⌐⌐⌐⌐⌐⌐⌐⌐⌐⌐⌐⌐⌐⌐⌐⌐

WHEN (AND WHERE) TO ASK FOR HELP

Couples who are thinking and talking about divorce, but haven't yet reached the point of no return, may benefit from marital therapy—both partners conferring jointly with one counselor. If marital counseling doesn't bring about a reconciliation, it will at least give both partners some badly needed perspective on the prospect of splitting up. Once a decision to divorce has become a reality, however, the issue of getting professional help takes on a different emotional tone.

How do you get help when you're facing divorce? There seem to be "planners" for everything: going to college, moving, getting married, having a formal party. In each case, a trained specialist can put it all together for you, from sending out the invitations to washing up the dishes. All you have to do is show up.

Whether fortunately or not, divorce is largely a do-it-yourself project; there is no such thing as a "divorce planner." Yet certain people and groups can help you through it—in ways that will not only ease the pain of the transition, but even reveal a more assured, competent, and well-balanced you. Asking for help may be the wisest thing you do throughout your entire divorce and recovery period.

You may want help only to cope with the initial trauma. Or you may manage to get through the immediate pain and shock, only to discover, after the papers are signed, that you're not functioning well and don't know how to get on with your life.

Why seek professional support? So you can take control over your life, rather than let divorce be something that *happens* to you.

Any of the traditional kinds of counselors—social workers, psychologists, psychotherapists, or psychiatrists—may specialize in counseling people who are going through divorce. (Sources of referral to such people are listed a little later in this chapter.)

For those whose divorces are complicated by other serious problems, such as alcoholism, drug addiction, or spouse abuse, special group programs have proved highly effective.

Hospitals and treatment centers also offer support programs. There are specific programs for women, for codependents (people with an unwholesome emotional dependence on someone or something), and for people struggling with depression or other psychiatric problems. Depending on your situation, one of these programs might be just what you need to help you cope with problems associated with your divorce.

REASONS FOR STAYING OR LEAVING

A person who is "codependent" may be unable to imagine living alone, even if his or her spouse is physically or verbally abusive. Thus, in many cases, the codependent will stick with an unhappy marriage rather than opt for the uncertainty of divorce. However, codependency doesn't always produce this outward marital stability. Sometimes a codependent will seek divorce precisely because the spouse isn't fulfilling his or her codependency needs.

Ruth, a 36-year-old schoolteacher, was the eldest daughter of an alcoholic father. During her childhood and adolescence she became quite capable and independent, often caring for her younger brothers when her mother and father were too embattled to function as parents. At the age of 28, Ruth married Bryce, a firm, decisive executive, and over the next eight years they had three children.

One day Ruth told Bryce she wanted a divorce. Stunned, Bryce asked why. Ruth said she resented him because he "wasn't vulnerable enough" for her. Without realizing it, she was emotionally programmed to cater to someone who was perpetually needy. Soon after the divorce, Ruth married a passive, depressed, alcoholic artist.

Ruth was a typical adult child of an alcoholic. Children who grow up in a household with an alcoholic parent learn to keep secrets and to bottle up their resentments. As Ruth expressed it during therapy, many years afterward, "I collected green stamps of resentment against Bryce. When I finally filled up the book, I traded it in—and traded him in."

WHAT'S A CODEPENDENT?

You may have encountered the term "codependent" and wondered what it meant. Originally coined to describe the spouse of an alcoholic, it's now understood to mean anyone who tries, desperately but unsuccessfully, to achieve safety and self-worth by clinging to someone or something.

Codependents, who sabotage themselves through self-destructive behavior, are likely to put up with physical or psychological abuse from their spouse rather than bail out of a bad marriage. If you are in a codependent relationship, you're never really at ease because you're preoccupied with questions of *compliance* and *control*.

Compliance issues include any of these:

- Valuing others' opinions and feelings more than your own
- Feeling deep down that nothing you do is ever good enough
- Compromising your own values and integrity to avoid someone else's anger or rejection

Control issues might include:

- Believing that most other people are incapable of taking care of themselves
- Anticipating other people's needs, and meeting those needs before they're even expressed
- Thinking of yourself as totally unselfish and completely devoted to other people's well-being

Early in life, children of alcoholics learn three basic rules for living: (1) Don't talk. (2) Don't feel. (3) Don't trust. Hemmed into this triangle of behavior, they fail to learn how to solve interpersonal problems. Often it takes psychotherapy, and/or a self-help group, to teach them more constructive patterns of relating to others.

DIVORCE SUPPORT GROUPS: WHAT THEY'RE ABOUT

Most recently, a new approach to divorce help has been initiated in a few communities. Called Divorce Anonymous, it's modeled after the approach of Alcoholics Anonymous. Members of a Divorce Anonymous group share a common affliction—divorce—and bring experience, understanding, and encouragement to one another in their common effort to overcome their problems.

The first Divorce Anonymous groups were started by Christine Archambault and Tasha Schaal in 1987. Both women had been through unusually difficult divorces; one had been beaten by her husband, and the other had been threatened by her husband with a gun. Both were emotionally scarred and in great need of support. The resourceful Ms. Schaal, who tried various groups (battered women's groups, AA, Alanon, Adult Children of Alcoholics) in search of emotional support, eventually concluded that the comprehensive 12-step approach could apply to recovery from divorce, too.

The great strength of such groups is that their members are all going through the same basic experience, regardless of how different the individual stories may be. Even though a therapist or counselor has the training and experience to help you look at your divorce objectively, you get a unique lift from meeting "regular people" who know *from personal experience* just what you're going through.

In general, a Divorce Anonymous meeting begins with each person talking briefly about his or her own experience. Participants describe where they are in the recovery process, and what they have learned so far that might be helpful to others. Then the meeting opens to discussion, with the leader calling on one person at a time. As in AA, people introduce themselves by first name only. The idea is that, although these individuals are in many ways unique, what's important in this situation is what they have in common. Sometimes the meeting focuses on a single topic: what happened at the lawyer's this week; how the children are taking it; how to deal with fears of abandonment or betrayal; starting new relationships; how to date; how to learn to trust again. But even in a single-topic meeting, there's usually time set aside to allow anyone to air an acute problem or an immediate emotional crisis.

IN THE COMPANY OF EQUALS

There's considerable healing power in encountering others who know *exactly* how you feel, and who are obviously recovering from divorce in a positive way. Also, there's nothing quite like being able to speak openly and honestly, in a room where no one will judge or criticize because everyone is or has been in the same situation. Group discussions provide a baseline against which you can measure your progress. In a given meeting, you can see that the problem that was troubling you last week is largely resolved, and that you've moved on to something else. Often, too, group discussions will give you insight into something said or done in your family that didn't seem significant at the time. A support group meeting is a safe and helpful place to pursue self-knowledge, and to practice understanding and forgiveness.

We can't say too often or too strongly that it's a proof of strength when you seek out the help you need. It's neither a confession of weakness nor an admission of illness. Divorce, one of life's most stressful and painful events, exacts a high emotional toll. Seeking professional help during divorce is an intelligent, mature decision. It shows that you're doing everything you can to take care of yourself. It helps ensure that you will handle your part of the divorce in a reasonable, responsible way, with the best guidance available.

GETTING HELP: CAN YOUR SPOUSE USE IT AGAINST YOU?

Many people are frightened away from getting the help they desperately need—not only because they're afraid to say, "I can't do it all alone," but because they've heard horror stories about what happens in divorce court when one spouse has received therapy or counseling. Attorneys may warn that if you go to a therapist "the other side" will use it against you, insinuating that you're mentally ill, that you shouldn't have custody of the children, that your emotional instability is the root cause of the divorce, and so on. Husbands and wives have indeed been known to use this as a weapon against each other. One spouse says, in effect, "You're crazy; I don't have to give you any money," or, "You shouldn't get custody of the children; you're *sick*." Unfortunately, the legal handling of some divorces fosters this type of hostility.

Be reassured, however, that getting help is widely recognized as a positive step. Having seen a counselor will actually help you to show mature and reasonable behavior and attitudes in conferences or court hearings. In addition, any reliable therapist will be glad to affirm that you sought help precisely to cope with the emotional crisis of divorce—and that for anyone in your situation, seeking sympathy, support, and guidance is an entirely reasonable and appropriate move.

RECOVERING YOUR SPIRITUAL BALANCE

If you understand "spirit" to mean the part of yourself that gravitates toward wholeness, integrity, and fulfillment, then you'll agree that the breakup of a long-term relationship is a spiritual crisis. While you are married, your connection with your spouse helps define your relationship to everyone and everything else in the world. Divorce, with its rupture and pain, shifts you into another plane of existence. Literally and figuratively, you are disoriented; your spiritual life is in disarray. If you've been brought up in a religious tradition, it may seem to you that God has betrayed or forgotten you. If you have no specific religious tradition to lean on, you may simply experience an existential void. Either way, your spirit needs care and nourishment.

This is no time to stop attending church or temple. If you have been active in your religious life, *stay* active. Religious institutions, after all, are there to help people through life crises—and the rupture of divorce is a crisis of first magnitude. Members of the clergy, who have lots of practice ministering to people in crisis, are often an excellent source of spiritual help. They can help you as you search to regain your lost sense of connectedness and spiritual integrity.

Once the news of your divorce gets out, some members of your congregation will be sympathetic and understanding, and others will probably be less helpful—but that's natural. As with relatives and friends, people in your congregation will vary in their ability to adapt to the changes you're going through.

If you've never been a practicing member of any faith, this may be the time for you to discover the spiritual side of life. Give religion a chance to take hold. Try attending services or discussion groups. Also, volunteer a little of your time to a faith-related activity such as a shelter for the homeless, thrift shop, or soup kitchen. Doing something for others will keep you from focusing exclusively on yourself. In addition, working alongside other volunteers is a superb way to meet people and get to know them.

Remember, too, that all twelve-step self-help programs (such as Alcoholics Anonymous, Narcotics Anonymous, Gamblers Anonymous, Al-Anon, and Divorce Anonymous) are built around a framework of spiritual development. In fact, Alcoholics Anonymous, the original self-help movement, mentions spiritual values or spiritual striving in fully nine of its twelve steps to recovery. This doesn't imply that twelve-step programs are necessarily "religious"—it simply means that they acknowledge and encourage spiritual reflection.

When you're coping with divorce, a spiritual outlook helps replace anguish and turmoil with calm and perspective. Personal honesty and integrity, fidelity to the truth, trust in a "higher power" or in your particular understanding of God—all these are paths toward healing. They can lead you back to a state of emotional health and wholeness that you may not have experienced since childhood.

To help as many people as possible, we've compiled an extensive list—but by no means an exhaustive list—of potential resources at the end of this book. Don't be afraid to consult this list of resources—and even more importantly, don't be afraid to use it.

9

⌐⌐⌐⌐⌐⌐⌐⌐⌐⌐⌐⌐⌐⌐⌐⌐⌐⌐

REMARRIED—WITH CHILDREN?

Almost seven million American children live in stepfamilies. New stepfamilies are forming at the rate of 6,000 a week. It's estimated that as many as one-third of all children born during the 1980s will live with a stepparent before the age of 18.

And while the divorce rate for first marriages is now about 50 percent, the rate for second marriages that include stepchildren is about 60 percent. Almost half of all stepparents who divorce do so within the first four years of the remarriage. The conclusion is inescapable: Few people who remarry with children realize the tremendous difficulties they face in forming a second family.

"In a remarriage with children, you are bringing two cultures together," says Patricia Papernow, a clinical psychologist in Cambridge, Massachusetts who specializes in stepfamily counseling. "All of a sudden you're slammed together. Everything is up for grabs, from how you celebrate Christmas to the size of the kids' allowances, how much television viewing is appropriate and whether it's okay to leave wet towels on the bathroom floor.

"These seemingly small details are the threads holding our daily lives together, and it feels as though our lives are unraveling."*

Just as grief and divorce go through stages of change and development, so does the formation of a new family. In stepfamilies, the changes are especially difficult because the remarrying

---

*Libman, Joan: "Step-by-Step; Remarriages Are Creating Complex Families With Problems 'The Brady Bunch' Never Faced." *Los Angeles Times*, Jan. 5, 1990. p. E-1.

couple and the children are experiencing very different feelings. In the beginning, these feelings may be very much in conflict.

COUPLE VS CHILDREN: CONFLICTING POINTS OF VIEW

During the stage of dating and falling in love, the couple feel only happiness and optimism. They are going through the exciting and energizing experience of getting to know each other, and they're gaining strength, confidence and happiness from the positive responses they give each other. They begin to share fantasies, dreams, and hopes for the future. They start to extend their social networks. They meet each other's extended family members and friends, whose support and encouragement strengthen their relationship.

But while the parents are enjoying all these positive experiences, what are the children feeling? Nothing very reassuring. They fear that they'll lose the devotion of the parent who's so blissfully in love. They distinctly resent this stranger who's intruding into what's left of their family. Their fantasies of reconciliation between their natural parents evaporate as the remarriage starts to seem possible, then probable.

Not surprisingly, the children often "don't like" the potential new partner. Their response may have nothing to do with the person's likability or good qualities, which may be considerable. In other circumstances, perhaps the kids would like this individual enormously. However, it's hard for them to see a real person behind all the negative feelings that an interloper conjures up.

STAGE TWO: RECOGNIZING THE PROBLEMS

Once the remarriage takes place, the family enters the second stage of creating a stepfamily. Social scientists and therapists used to assume that a stepfamily was very much like an ordinary nuclear family. It's now clear, however, that the differences are great and complex.

In first marriages, adults and children "grow up together." They get to know each other bit by bit, forming patterns of behavior, learning to resolve differences, and establishing family traditions. They gradually learn each others' habits and quirks,

STEPFAMILIES EVERYWHERE

With divorce and remarriage so common in American society, stepfamily life is an everyday reality for millions of adults and children. Consider:

- Overall, the divorce rate in the U.S.A. is 50 percent.
- Among remarried couples with children from previous marriages, the divorce rate is 60 percent.
- As many as one-third of children born during the 1980s may live with a stepparent by the age of 18.
- Remarried people consider stepchildren the biggest source of difficulty in their new marriage.
- A stepfamily needs anywhere from *two to seven years* to stabilize.

and they have time to adjust to and tolerate one another. They undergo change side by side as members of a cooperating group. They're linked together by powerful psychological forces.

The stepfamily, by contrast, is a group of strangers with conflicting loyalties of varying strength. Since stepfamily members don't have that long infancy-to-childhood period of getting acquainted and adjusted, they face numerous obstacles to closeness and acceptance. The children's relationships with the adults are lopsided—intense with the biological parent; wary, suspicious, perhaps hostile toward the newcomer. Even in natural families, children instinctively know how to play one parent off against the other; stepfamily life greatly exaggerates the opportunities and the motivation to do this. The new parents simultaneously face two difficult jobs—forming a new marriage and forming a new family. These jobs often clash.

To make matters especially difficult, the newly remarried parents—in their happiness and optimism—typically harbor fantasies of stepfamily harmony and joy. Usually these fantasies are far removed from the realities of stepfamily life. Yet the new spouses' happiness with each other initially blinds them to their children's misery.

In the second marriage, the honeymoon may be very brief. Before long, the spouses wake up to reality. They recognize that

WHAT PARENTS BELIEVE ABOUT STEPFAMILIES

What remarried people believe about stepfamilies stems largely from what they believe about family life in general. It clears the air if the spouses are able to articulate, from the outset, what they think the norms for their new stepfamily should be.

Warning: A stepfather who thinks his new stepchildren should immediately be as loving, respectful, and loyal to him as to their biological father is bound for disappointment. He may blame his new wife for having reared children who don't measure up to his expectations.

Naturally, the reverse is true, too: a stepmother whose new stepchildren dislike or disrespect her may blame the situation on her husband's way of handling his kids. Overall, however, more men than women complain that relations with their stepchildren are a source of difficulty.

something is not quite right, or even that something is seriously wrong. They begin to realize that this marriage is very different from the romantic idyll of a first marriage.

STAGE THREE: FACING THE MUSIC

Ideally, the stepfamily members realize love and hope are not sufficient to create a healthy new family; they begin to recognize problems, understand them, and work together to solve them. New rules and routines are necessary. People have to adapt to one another and to the new situation; there is no "going on as before."

Eventually, the stepfamily that does its adjustment work diligently, lovingly, and intelligently enters the final stage of adjustment. They learn to resolve conflicts. Each member has a place within the stepfamily. Relationships become more intimate, trusting, and comfortable. A sense of stepfamily tradition and history gradually develops.

STRENGTHENING THE MARRIAGE FIRST

It takes from two to seven years to achieve this "ideal" adjustment, according to Marilyn and Ed Winter-Tamkin, stepfamily specialists in Santa Fe, New Mexico.

Rule Number One, the Winter-Tamkins say, is to work toward being a couple. You *must* cement your own relationship with each other before you can deal with relationships with the children.

Your strong and obvious love and respect for each other will send a clear message to the children: this is real, good, and lasting, and it's what you're going to live with. Presenting a genuine unity to the children will stifle their instinctive impulse toward sabotage. No matter how much they may like your new partner, the children (whether they know it or not) have an underlying wish to put things back the way they were before.

A deep and true partnership will show the children a better example of adult love than they may have seen in your first marriage. It will reassure them that you are not helpless, lonely, or defeated by your divorce.

According to the Winter-Tamkins, "Those couples who have the best chance for creating a successful stepfamily are those who plan ahead, understand stepfamily dynamics, are able to communicate well, and are committed to making their stepfamilies work."

BEWARE OF "BLENDING"

The single word that seems to foster the most trouble in forming stepfamilies is the misnomer "blended family." This pop term creates false expectations of what should happen. It makes stepparents try to do what experts feel is the worst thing they could possibly do—"blend" everyone together into one homogenized mass.

So Rule Number Two is not to force "togetherness." The biological parent in the stepfamily has to juggle two conflicting needs:

On the one hand, to give added love and time to the children to counteract their natural fear that this parent—like the one who moved out after the divorce—also may be taken away from them;

On the other hand, to establish the new marriage, build closeness and solidity for the future, and become part of a real "couple."

The stepparent needs to form a bond with the stepchildren—but may resent the attention this requires, since it interferes with building the new marriage.

Although it takes an enormous amount of energy and organization, it's essential to establish schedules and patterns of family activity that allow the newly married couple to be alone together at times, away from the children. It's equally vital that the new schedule give the children their needed share of being together by turn with the whole family, the biological parent, and the stepparent.

INSTANT PARENT: NO SUCH THING

The idea that the new stepparent should become an "instant parent," and that the newly married couple should immediately be able to function smoothly as coparents, is unrealistic, judging by the experience of real stepfamilies.

As a stepparent, no matter what you do and no matter how "good" you are, you will never actually replace the original parent. Although you *can* create a completely separate and unique relationship with stepchildren, stepping into a biological parent's shoes is the one thing you should not attempt to do.

As the biological parent, you can't relate to your new partner as if he or she were your children's other natural parent. It takes years for a married couple to develop good patterns of parenting together. (Some parents never do; they're in conflict over childrearing throughout the children's growing up!)

How much harder, then, for a biological parent to adjust to coparenting with a new partner who isn't used to your ways of handling the children's problems, and who isn't yet an integral part of the family. How much harder for a stepparent to walk into a family where relationships and behavior patterns were long established, recently underwent major adjustments to accommodate the realities of divorce, and are now undergoing another readjustment!

The most common mistake that stepparents make—and that their new marriage partners often haplessly encourage them to

PARENTS WHO DON'T HAVE CUSTODY

What about the divorced parent who doesn't get custody? If it's the mother, no matter whether she relinquished custody for practical, financial, or psychological reasons, people tend to assume the worst—"What did she do that was bad enough to make her lose her children?"

Of course, some mothers deservedly lose custody of their children. But it's time to change the common assumption that the noncustodial parent is necessarily the "bad parent."

In some parts of the country, support groups exist for parents without custody. These groups help noncustodial parents regain self-esteem and realize that they are still important to their children.

make—is plunging into the parent role too quickly, expecting immediate affection and respect from the stepchildren. A far wiser approach is to think of the relationship with the stepchildren as if it were the beginning of an adult friendship. Nobody expects immediate loyalty, acceptance and obedience from a brand-new acquaintance. Friendships unfold step by step, item by item. Communication becomes more intimate day by day. Friends spend small amounts of time together at first, then larger amounts more frequently. They observe and respect each other's privacy. They keep their demands minor in the beginning, letting the give-and-take reach its own level as the friendship matures.

Eagerness to dive right in is understandable. The stepparent needs to be accepted and loved by the children—after all, they come with the marriage, and can come between the two spouses if things don't work out right. The biological parent has a deep need for the children's approval of the new marriage partner. Everybody wants things to be "normal" right away. Most people find it hard to live in transition; people like things to be settled, secure. Being patient and holding back at this time is hard and uncomfortable, but necessary.

With patience, tolerance, and a high degree of respect for the children's individual needs and personalities, remarried parents

STEPFAMILY: THE CYCLE FOR CHILDREN

Growing up is hard enough; coping with a new stepparent, and possibly a new stepbrother or -sister, makes the job even rougher. Several million American children either have experienced, or will experience, the following cycle:

1. Their own natural parents' marriage deteriorates and finally breaks up.
2. They adjust to the breakup, and in many cases resign themselves to seeing one of their parents seldom or never.
3. The parent with whom they live starts dating, and enters into a serious new relationship.
4. The parent marries the new person. Perhaps the new person brings along children from his or her previous marriage.
5. The new couple has a baby—another addition to the family.
6. Unresolved stresses wear everyone down, and eventually cause the second marriage to break up.
7. Once again, they go through the trauma of divorce and a prolonged period of readjustment.

can get their marriage on a solid footing and the stepparent can build a rewarding and satisfying relationship with the children. It will *not* be the same kind of relationship a biological parent has with his or her children. It will have its own qualities and its own rewards. It can be most quickly achieved and best appreciated if it's recognized for exactly what it is, not forced to conform to some other ideal.

HOW KIDS FEEL TOWARD STEPPARENTS

Some children may actually prefer a stepparent over their natural parent because the stepparent is more honest, more loving, more attentive, more of an ally, a better role model. But they never emotionally discard the biological parent, and they continue to make a sharp distinction between the two. Even children who are very young at the time of remarriage make this strong distinction. Loyalty to the biological parent stays intact throughout life, even when animosity between the divorced spouses remains high.

One 20-year-old described by Judith Wallerstein in her 10-year study of divorced families had an excellent relationship with his stepfather, yet his feelings about his biological father were still profound many years after the divorce.

"You don't understand," he explained. "My stepfather could be Saint Benedict or Saint Francis. He could walk on water, and it would not change the hurt I feel about my dad."

The most important thing stepparents can do in the beginning is to "function like an aunt or babysitter," Dr. James H. Bray of Baylor College of Medicine in Houston concluded after seven years of studying stepfamilies. "Discipline should be left to the biological parent."

Of course, it must be understood that when the biological parent is absent, the stepparent will fill the parental role. The new couple need to reach the best possible agreement on what the ground rules are. At the beginning, the stepparent may have to adjust or even stifle natural impulses to be stricter or more lenient than the biological parent. Eventually, if new spouses work conscientiously toward *being a couple*, they can come to an understanding and an agreement on how to handle discipline and other problems with children.

An additional rule—one that can be applied throughout all the stages of divorce, remarriage, and recovery—is this: Remember that you're only human. When you goof, forgive yourself.

WHAT CAN GO WRONG BETWEEN STEPSIBLINGS

In a stepfamily, children from two different biological families often find themselves at loggerheads. Here are a few of the common hurdles:

Kids get territorial. A child who was always easygoing before the remarriage may suddenly become possessive in ways the parents never anticipated. Perhaps he now has to share a room with a sibling or stepsibling; suddenly he feels that, because of the remarriage, his room is being invaded.

Chuck wore neon sneakers, put orange "fun color" in his hair, chewed a whole pack of gum at a time, and watched music videos with the volume turned all the way up. Ned wore polo shirts and loafers, read voraciously, and spent hours every week practicing on his clarinet. When these two boys learned they would have to share a bedroom, their jaws dropped. They might as well have come from different planets.

Kids get displaced in rank. Suddenly an "eldest child" loses her seniority, and much of her identity along with it. Suddenly the "baby of the family" has a younger stepsibling who steals the limelight.

Geraldine had always been the one to watch her little brother when her mother went out to the store. Now her stepsister Wanda, two years older and a foot taller, was being left in charge of everything whenever Mom went out, and collecting all the money for babysitting. Worse yet, Geraldine suspected she was going to be in line for Wanda's horrible hand-me-down clothes.

The kids are subjected to two different sets of parental goals. It takes years to instill values in a child. Divorce and remarriage mean the child has to absorb a whole new set of values.

From kindergarten on, Farid had understood that he was destined for college and then graduate school. But his new stepfather didn't seem to take that dream seriously. He balked at paying for weekend and summer enrichment programs. He spoke derisively of "eggheads." He even kept the TV on high volume at night when Farid was trying to study.

The grandparents don't treat everyone alike. Even when they're trying to do their best, grandparents, aunts and uncles, and other relatives may goof. Sometimes, unfortunately, they're actively hostile.

Nancy was prepared to like Carolyn, her new stepsister—or at least to give her a fair chance. But within a month, Carolyn was invited to spend a weekend with her own grandmother. She came back with a suntan, two complete new outfits, and ticket stubs from a fancy theater production. Nancy, who had spent the weekend cleaning her room and babysitting, felt totally outclassed.

The noncustodial parent causes trouble. When a noncustodial parent sees his children functioning within a new "intact" family, he may seethe with resentment and anger.

George thought he had accepted that his two children now had a new family life with their mother, a stepfather, and two stepsiblings. But when he learned that his ex-wife and her new husband had put all four children in parochial school, he was beside himself. He had always hated organized religion, and he wanted his children to think for themselves. When he went to pick up his two kids for a visit, the first thing he said was, "Well, have the nuns totally brainwashed you?"

NOBODY'S PERFECT

The readjustment period in stepfamilies is so difficult and complex that nobody can be expected to handle it with ease, confidence, and efficiency—let alone perfection. You may have made up your mind never to interfere with your partner's way of disciplining your stepchildren—but one day they get on your nerves so much, you yell at her to stop coddling them, and you give them a good swat on their backsides. Or you get so sick of hearing your stepchildren praise their "real" mother that one day you yell, "Well, if she's so great, go live with *her*," and slam the door behind you as you storm out of the house. One day you feel as if you have had kids up to *here* and never get five minutes alone with your wife; you tell her if you'd known it was going to be like this, you never would have taken on her bunch of brats. One day, after playing peacemaker and go-between and housemother to your new husband and your own kids without getting any cooperation from any of them, you blow your top and say, "Go ahead, all of you, just fight it out!"

It's bound to happen. There's only one thing to do. Go back, say you were wrong. Remind everyone gently that you haven't had much experience or practice being a stepparent (or being married to a stepparent). Ask for another chance, and perhaps for a little patience on their part.

Never add the word "but." Don't say, "But you kids get on my nerves!" or, "But if you hadn't done this, I wouldn't have done that." Just take responsibility for your part. Maybe with your good example the kids will examine their own consciences, and start taking a little responsibility for their behavior.

THE GREENHORN STEPPARENT

All of the adjustments of the newly-formed stepfamily are that much harder if the stepparent has never had children of his or her own. There are no training schools for parents except the school of hard experience; parenthood is all on-the-job training. But biological parents get to learn slowly, starting with a tiny infant who doesn't talk back yet, and coping with the hard parts gradually, day by day, year by year. The formerly childless stepparent starts from zero, with no benefit of experience— confronting stepchildren who are apt to feel hostile rather than loyal and loving. For "greenhorn" stepparents, the rule about not jumping in feet first will make things much easier on everyone.

EPILOGUE:
AN ENDING AND A BEGINNING

Remember that, although divorce is the end of your marriage, it's also the beginning of a new life. What you make of that life is up to you. You can stay mired in remorse, regrets, and recrimination, or you can leave the past behind and strike out in a fresh new direction. The choice is yours.

Throughout this book on recovery from divorce, we've emphasized that, even if it was your partner and not you who initiated the divorce, you need not play the role of the helpless victim of circumstances. At every turn of the divorce process, you'll be faced with decisions. *Make* those decisions; don't let someone else make them for you. Keep certain facts in mind:

- **Divorce Causes Emotional Turmoil.** Whether or not you're the initiator of the divorce, you can expect to feel some measure of fear, sorrow, anger, depression, and confusion as the structure of your married life disintegrates. The turmoil is unpleasant, but it's normal.

- **You and Your Spouse Have Very Different Adjustment Problems.** If you're the initiator of the divorce, you have the upper hand at first, since you have mentally "worked up a case" against your spouse. However, you may later suffer from self-doubt, guilt, and remorse. If you're the noninitiator, taken by surprise, you're at a disadvantage at first, suffering from shock, hurt, and a sense of betrayal. However, you may later gain considerable strength through anger, indignation, and your growing determination to survive this ordeal.

129

- **You will need to look inward for strength to cope with the crisis of divorce.** Therapists, support groups, mediators— all can help, but none can "fix" your personal divorce problems. You yourself will have to assess the situation, make decisions, and then (the hardest part!) follow through. The strength you need is there within you. Your task is to find it and tap into it, as often and as deeply as you need to.

- **You Can't Spare the Children Completely.** Don't fool yourself into thinking that because your children aren't saying much, they're taking the divorce lightly. Even if your family life has been wretched, your children deeply need both of their parents. For their sake, keep this in mind when you and your spouse work out the custody arrangements.

A FEW WORDS OF ADVICE

There is no blueprint for the perfect divorce; dissolving a marriage is largely a do-it-yourself project. However, it's wise to heed these few recommendations:

- *When you and your spouse have agreed to split up, find separate housing at the earliest possible opportunity.* Continuing to live under the same roof is sometimes advised for legal reasons, but it's *never* advised for emotional reasons. Even if it means a big drop in your standard of living, find separate quarters for yourselves somehow.

- *Make a decision not to go to war.* Lawyers will find it natural to pit you and your spouse against each other in a legal battle. All-out legal war quickly gets expensive, and in the end the lawyers are the only winners. If possible, arrange with your spouse to consult a divorce mediator. Agreeing on global settlement principles will make subsequent legal negotiations easier and less bitter.

- *Get emotional as well as legal help.* Talk out your troubles with a trusted counselor, a support group, friends, or all of these. Bottled-up emotions won't disappear; they'll pop out later in some hard-to-control form such as depression, anxiety, phobias, or paranoia.

- *Get emotional help for your children, not just for yourself.*

It's the rare kid who can say, "I'm so upset and depressed about my parents' divorce that I can't even function." Instead, a kid will probably express unhappiness through action—becoming nervous, "hyper," obsessive, sickly, accident-prone, obnoxious, or delinquent. Regular contact with a counselor or therapist can help your youngster cope. Remember, just because *you* are starting to feel somewhat better about the divorce doesn't mean your child is, too.

■ *Decide which old relationships you want to preserve.* Realize that some of your friends will probably drop you because they're uncomfortable with your divorce. Tell yourself that's *their* problem, not yours, and be open to new friendships. Realize also that your in-laws may still like you and want your company, even if your ex-spouse doesn't. How you handle this depends on how you feel about the in-laws. If you like, it may be possible to maintain cordial contact indefinitely.

■ *Expect your complete recovery to take years.* No one really recovers quickly and easily from a divorce. That's because recovery is a learning process, and learning takes time. You'll need time to get over your anger and sorrow, time to be lonely, time to organize new living arrangements, time to make new friends, and—if you eventually remarry and children are involved—time to adjust to the difficult problems of stepparenting.

THE GREAT HEALER

When all is said and done, the key to recovering from divorce is the healing power of time. But don't expect to sit back and let time do all the work for you. Approaching your divorce intelligently and thoughtfully is the best way to lend a hand to time. No matter what happens, you should know that you do have within you the strength, courage, and spirit to survive divorce and make a complete recovery. Your primary task is to search, and keep searching, until you find those inner resources. We hope this book can help.

፼፼፼፼፼፼፼፼፼፼፼፼፼፼፼

RESOURCES FOR PEOPLE RECOVERING FROM DIVORCE

Divorce recovery is a process that runs on its own schedule. In the early stages, you may be too hurt, angry, or confused to feel like looking for help. As times goes on, however, you'll probably feel the desire to reach out and connect with others whose experience in some way parallels your own.

This list of resources may include a group of people who can help you feel better about yourself, your divorce, and your life.* Take a look at the list and decide where your interests lie—then make a phone call. You have nothing to lose, and perhaps a great deal to gain. (Consult your local directory for organizations or groups in your area.)

ALCOHOL PROBLEMS

Adult Children of Alcoholics (founded 1984)
P.O. Box 3216
Torrance, CA 90505
(213) 534-1815

Al-Anon Family Groups (founded 1951)
P.O. Box 862, Midtown Station
New York, NY 10018-0862
(212) 302-7240

---

*Please note that this list does not include every organization that deals with the various aspects of divorce. Furthermore, inclusion on this list does not constitute endorsement by the authors or publishers of this book.

Alcoholics Anonymous (founded 1935)
Box 459, Grand Central Station
New York, NY 10163
(212) 686-1100

Calix Society (founded 1947)
7601 Wayzata Blvd.
Minneapolis, MN 55426
(612) 546-0544
Spiritual program for people maintaining their sobriety.

Jewish Alcoholics, Chemically Dependent Persons & Significant Others (J.A.C.S.) (founded 1980)
197 East Broadway, Room 308
New York, NY 10002
(212) 473-4747

Secular Organizations for Sobriety (SOS) (founded 1986)
P.O. Box 5
Buffalo, NY 14215-0005
(716) 834-2921
Help for alcoholics and addicts who want to acknowledge their
disease and maintain sobriety as a separate issue from religion
or spirituality.

COUNSELING AND PSYCHOTHERAPY

National Association of Social Workers
7981 Eastern Ave.
Silver Spring, MD 20910
(800) 638-8799
In Maryland call (800) 648-0976
Ask for a listing of social workers in your area, as published in
the most recent Register of Clinical Social Workers. Published
every two years, the register lists some 20,000 social workers.

American Psychiatric Association
1400 K Street N.W.
Washington, D.C. 20005
(202) 682-6000
This office will give you the phone number of your local
American Psychiatric Association society, which can refer you to
psychiatrists in your area.

National Register of Health Service Providers in Psychology
1730 Rhode Island Avenue N.W.
Suite 1200
Washington, D.C. 20036
(202) 833-2377
To get names of licensed psychologists in your area, ask at a
library reference desk for the latest edition of the *National
Register of Health Service Providers in Psychology*. The register, which is updated regularly, lists more than 16,000 psychologists.

DIVORCE MEDIATION

Academy of Family Mediators
P.O. Box 10501
Eugene, OR 97440
(503) 345-1205

American Arbitration Association
140 West 51st Street
New York, NY 10020
(212) 484-4000

American Bar Association
Standing Committee on Dispute Resolution
1800 M St. N.W.
Washington, DC 20036
(202) 331-2258

Divorce and Family Mediators
37 Arch Street
Greenwich, CT 06830
(203) 622-5900

Divorce Mediation Research Project
1720 Emerson Street
Denver, CO 80218
(303) 447-8116
Publishers of the Directory of Mediation Services.

Family Center for Mediation and Counseling
3514 Players Mill Road
Kensington, MD 20895
(301) 946-3400

DIVORCE SUPPORT

North American Association of Separated and Divorced Catholics
(founded 1975)
1100 S. Goodman Street
Rochester, NY 14620
(716) 271-1320

Divorce Anonymous (founded 1987)
2600 Colorado Ave., Suite 270
Santa Monica, CA 90404
(213) 315-6538

The Friends (founded 1971)
P.O. Box 389
Fargo, ND 58107
(701) 235-7341
A "bank" of people who have been through various life crises,
who are matched with someone undergoing a similar problem.

The Single Life (founded 1972)
85 Central Street
Waltham, MA 02154
(617) 891-3750
A support organization of divorced, separated, widowed, and
never-married men and women.

DIVORCE: LEGAL RESOURCES

Center for Women Policy Studies
2000 P Street, N.W., Suite 508
Washington, DC 20036
(202) 872-1770
Newsletter on family violence, legislative and program advocacy.

Child Custody Project
American Bar Association
1800 M St., N.W.
Washington, DC 20036
(202) 331-2200
Written material, parent, lawyer, and judicial education.

Child Custody Project
Women's Legal Defense Fund
2000 P Street, N.W., Suite 400
Washington, DC 20036
(202) 887-0364
List of publications, newsletter, legal advocacy, referrals.

Children's Defense Fund
122 C Street, N.W., Suite 400
Washington, DC 20001
(202) 628-8787
Newsletter, legal advocacy, legislative advocacy, referrals.

The Children's Foundation
815 15th Street, N.W., Suite 928
Washington, DC 20005
(202) 347-3300
Newsletter, legislative and policy advocacy.

Committee for Mother & Child Rights, Inc. (founded 1980)
Rt. 1, Box 256 A
Clear Brook, VA 22624
(703) 722-3652
Information and support for mothers with custody problems.

The Divorce Support Center
370 Central Ave.
Mountainside, NJ 07902
(201) 233-1717

National Center for Women and Family Law
799 Broadway, Room 402
New York, NY 10003
(212) 674-8200
List of publications, newsletter, assistance to lower-income women, legal service offices.

National Women's Law Center
1616 P Street, N.W.
Washington, DC 20036
(202) 328-5160
Newsletter, analysis of legislation and policy, monitoring of agency compliance with the law.

NOW Legal Defense and Education Fund
99 Hudson Street
New York, NY 10013
(212) 925-6635
Newsletter, legislative and legal advocacy, referrals.

Recommended Reading

How to Do Your Own Divorce in California, 10th Edition.
Berkeley, CA: Nolo Press, 1983.

DRUG ABUSE

Cocaine Anonymous (founded 1982)
P.O. Box 1367
Culver City, CA 90232
(800) 347-8988

Drugs Anonymous (formerly Pills Anonymous)
P.O. Box 473, Ansonia Station
New York, NY 10023
(212) 874-0700

800-COCAINE
P.O. Box 100
Summit, NJ 07901
(800) 262-2463
National drug abuse treatment referral and information service.

Families Anonymous (founded 1971)
P.O. Box 528
Van Nuys, CA 91408
(818) 989-7841
Fellowship of relatives and friends of people involved in abuse
of mind-altering substances, or exhibiting related behavioral
problems.

Nar-Anon (founded 1971)
Nar-Anon Family Group Headquarters
P.O. Box 2562
Palos Verdes, CA 90274-0119
(213) 547-5800
For relatives and friends concerned about drug abuse.

Narcotics Anonymous (founded 1953)
P.O. Box 9999
Van Nuys, CA 91409
(818) 780-3951

EATING AND BODY IMAGE

National Association to Aid Fat Americans (founded 1969)
P.O. Box 745
Westbury, NY 11590
(718) 217-8623
For thsoe who think people should have the right to exist with happiness and dignity regardless of their size.

Overeaters Anonymous (founded 1960)
P.O. Box 29870
Los Angeles, CA 90009
(213) 542-8363
Fellowship for people who want to stop eating compulsively.

EMOTIONAL PROBLEMS

Depressives Anonymous (founded 1977)
329 East 62nd Street
New York, NY 10021
(212) 689-2600 (answering service only)

Emotions Anonymous (founded 1971)
P.O. Box 4245
St. Paul, MN 55104
(612) 647-9712
For people with emotional problems.

National Depressive & Manic-Depressive Association (founded 1986)
53 West Jackson Boulevard
Chicago, IL 60604
(312) 939-2442
For depressive and manic-depressive people and their families.

GAMBLING

Gam-Anon Family Groups (founded 1960)
P.O. Box 157
Whitestone, NY 11357
(718) 352-1671
For family members and friends of compulsive gamblers.

Gamblers Anonymous (founded 1960)
P.O. Box 17173
Los Angeles, CA 90017
(213) 386-8789

MARRIAGE AND FAMILY

Association of Couples for Marriage Enrichment (founded 1973)
P.O. Box 10596
Winston-Salem, NC 27108
(919) 724-1526

Interace (founded 1983)
P.O. Box 582
Forest Hills, NY 11375-9998
(718) 657-2271
Support for interracial couples, their children, bi-racial adults,
and interracial adoptive families.

MENTAL ILLNESS

National Alliance for the Mentally Ill (founded 1979)
2101 Wilson Boulevard, Suite 302
Arlington, VA 22201-3008
(703) 524-7600
Support for relatives of the seriously mentally ill.

Parents Involved Network (founded 1984)
311 South Juniper Street, Room 902
Philadelphia, PA 19107
(215) 735-2465
For parents whose children have serious emotional problems.

Siblings and Adult Children's Network (founded 1982)
SAC Network/NAMI
2101 Wilson Boulevard, Suite 302
Arlington, VA 22201-3008
(703) 524-7600
For siblings and children of people with mental illness.

PHYSICAL AND EMOTIONAL ABUSE

Batterers Anonymous (founded 1979)
B.A. Press
1269 North E Street
San Bernardino, CA 92405
(714) 355-1100
Self-help for men who want to control their anger and stop their abusive behavior toward women.

National Domestic Violence Hotline
1-800-333-SAFE

Parents Anonymous (founded 1970)
6733 S. Sepulveda Boulevard, Suite 270
Los Angeles, CA 90045
(800) 421-0353
For parents who are, or fear they may become, out of control in disciplining their children.

Parents United (founded 1972)
P.O. Box 952
San Jose, CA 95108
(408) 453-7616
Support groups for parents whose children have been abused sexually. Also for adults who were sexually molested as children.

Sexual Assault Recovery Anonymous (S.A.R.A.) (founded 1983)
P.O. Box 16
Surrey, British Columbia, Canada V3T 4W4
Education and self-help for adults and adolescents who were sexually abused in childhood.

Victims of Child Abuse Laws (V.O.C.A.L.) (founded 1984)
1212 N. Broadway, Suite 133
Santa Ana, CA 92701
(714) 558-0200
Protecting the rights of people accused of child abuse. Also,

protecting children against abusers within the children's services system.

SINGLE PARENTING

Parents Without Partners
8807 Colesville Road
Silver Spring, MD 20910
(800) 637-7974 or (301) 588-9354
Support groups for single parents.

Single Mothers By Choice (founded 1981)
P.O. Box 1642, Gracie Square Station
New York, NY 10028
(212) 988-0993

Single Parent Resource Center (founded 1975)
1165 Broadway
New York, NY 10001
(212) 213-0047

Single Parents Society (NY and NJ)
527 Cinnaminson Avenue
Palmyra, NJ 08065
(609) 424-8872

The Sisterhood of Black Single Mothers, Inc. (founded 1974)
1360 Fulton St., Room 413
Brooklyn, NY 11216
(800) 338-3732

Women On Their Own, Inc. (W.O.T.O.) (founded 1982)
P.O. Box 1026
Willingboro, NJ 08046
(609) 871-1499
Support, networking, advocacy, quarterly newsletter. Loan program.

Recommended Reading

Edwards, Marie, and Hoover, Eleanor: *The Challenge of Being Single*. New York: New American Library, 1975.

Knight, Bryan: *Enjoying Single Parenthood*. New York: Van

Nostrand Reinhold, 1980.

Levine, James A.: *Who Will Raise the Children? New Options for Fathers*. New York: Bantam, 1977.

PARENTING

Stepfamily Association of America
215 Centennial Mall South, Suite 212
Lincoln, NE 68508
(402) 477-7837

Stepfamily Foundation (founded 1975)
333 West End Avenue
New York, NY 10023
(212) 877-3244
For those living in a step relationship.

Tough Love (founded 1980)
Box 1069
Doylestown, PA 18901
(215) 348-7090
For dealing with out-of-control behavior of a family member.

SELF-HELP CLEARINGHOUSES

American Self-Help Clearinghouse
St. Clare-Riverside Medical Center
Denville, NJ 07834
(201) 625-7101
In New Jersey: (800) 367-6274

Sacramento Self-Help Clearinghouse
Mental Health Association of Sacramento
5370 Elvos Avenue, Suite B
Sacramento, CA 95819
(916) 368-3100

San Francisco Self-Help Clearinghouse
Mental Health Association
2398 Pine Street

San Francisco, CA 94115
(415) 921-4401

Self-Help Center
1600 Dodge Avenue, Suite S-122
Evanston, IL 60201
(708) 328-0470

Self-Help Center
U.C.L.A.
Franz Hall, Room 2349
405 Hilgard Avenue
Los Angeles, CA 90024
(213) 825-1799
California only: (800) 222-LINK

Self-Help Clearinghouse of Merced County
Mental Health Association of Merced County
P.O. Box 343
Merced, CA 95341
(209) 723-8861

Recommended Reading

Barbach, Lonnie: *For Yourself: The Fulfillment of Female Sexuality.* New York: Doubleday, 1975.

Benson, Barbara, and Bova, Ben: *Survival Guide for the Suddenly Single.* New York: St. Martin's Press, 1980.

Braden, N.: *The Psychology of Romantic Love.* New York: Bantam, 1981

Hemlinger, Trudy: *After You've Said Goodbye: How to Recover After Ending a Relationship.* Cambridge, MA: Schenkman, 1980.

Kingma, Daphne Rose: *Coming Apart.* New York: Fawcett, 1989.

Singleton, Mary Ann: *Life After Marriage: Divorce as a New Beginning.* New York: Stein & Day, 1979.

Trafford, Abigail: *Surviving Divorce.* New York: Bantam, 1984.

Vaughan, Diane: *Uncoupling: Turning Points in Intimate Relationships.* New York: Oxford University Press, 1986.

Wassmer, Arthur C.: *Making Contact.* New York: Dial, 1978.

Zilbergeld, Bernie: *Male Sexuality.* New York: Bantam, 1978.

SOURCES

Ahrons, Constance R.: "The Continuing Coparental Relationship Between Divorced Spouses," *American Journal of Orthopsychiatry*, vol. 5, no. 3, July 1981.

American Association of Retired Persons: *Divorce After 50*. Washington, D.C.: American Association of Retired Persons, 1987.

Bass, Howard L. and Rein, M. L.: *Divorce or Marriage: A Legal Guide*. Englewood Cliffs, N.J.: Prentice-Hall, 1976.

Belli, Melvin, and Wilkinson, Allen P.: *Everybody's Guide to the Law*. New York: Gramercy, 1989.

Blumenthal, Monica D.: "Mental Health Among the Divorced," *Archives of General Psychiatry*, vol. 16, May 1967, pp. 603–608.

Bothwell, Sallye, and Weissman, Myrna M.: "Social Impairments Four Years After an Acute Depressive Episode," *American Journal of Orthopsychiatry*, vol. 47, no. 2, April 1977, pp. 231–37.

Briscoe, C. William, and Smith, James B.: "Depression and Marital Turmoil," *Archives of General Psychiatry*, vol. 29, December 1973, pp. 811–17.

Briscoe, C. William; Smith, James B.; Robbins, Eli, et al: "Divorce and Psychiatric Disease," *Archives of General Psychiatry*, vol. 29, July 1973, pp. 119–25.

Brody, Jane E.: "Divorce's Stress Exacts Long-Term Health Toll," *New York Times*, December 13, 1983, pp. C1, C5.

Cantor, Donald J.: *Escape From Marriage: How to Solve the Problems of Divorce*. New York: William Morrow, 1971.

Caplan, G.: "Guidance for Divorcing Parents," *Archives of Disease in Childhood*, vol. 62, 1987, pp. 752–53.

Cartwright, Rosalind D.; Lloyd, Stephen; Knight, Sara, and Trenholme, Irene: "Broken Dreams: A Study of the Effects of Divorce and Depression on Dream Content," *Psychiatry*, vol. 47, August 1984.

Clair, Bernard E.: *The Ex-Factor: The Complete Do-It-Yourself Post-Divorce Handbook*. New York: D.I. Fine, 1986.

Crytser, Ann: *The Wife-In-Law Trap*. Pocket Books, 1990.

De Angelis, Sidney M.: *You're Entitled! A Divorce Lawyer Talks to Women*. New York: Contemporary Books, 1989.

Doherty, William J., and Burge, Sandra K.: "Divorce Among Physicians," *Journal of the American Medical Association*, vol 261, no. 16, April 28, 1989, pp. 2374–77.

Finke, Nikki: "Nasty, Nasty, Nasty," *Los Angeles Times*, December 8, 1989, pp. E1,E8–E11.

Friedman, James T.: *The Divorce Handbook*. New York: Random House, 1984.

Gartner, Alan: *Help: A Working Guide to Self-Help Groups*. New York: New Viewpoints/Vision Books, 1980.

Gillis, Phyllis L.: *Days Like This: A Tale of Divorce*. New York: McGraw-Hill, 1986.

Glasner, Robert D., and Borduin, Charles M.: "Models of Divorce Therapy: An Overview," *American Journal of Psychotherapy*, vol. 40, no. 2, April 1986.

Harwood, Norma: *A Woman's Legal Guide to Separation and Divorce in All 50 States*. New York: Scribners, 1985.

Helmstetter, Shad: *The Self-Talk Solution*. New York: William Morrow, 1987.

Hoff, Patricia: *Parental Kidnapping: How To Prevent Abduction and What to Do if Your Child is Abducted*. National Center for Missing and Exploited Children, 1835 K St. N.W., Suite 700, Washington, D.C. 20006, 1985.

Jacobs, John W.: "Divorce and Child Custody Resolution: Conflicting Legal and Psychological Paradigms," *American Journal of Psychiatry*, vol. 143, no. 2, February 1986.

Jacobs, John W.: "Treatment of Divorcing Fathers: Social and Psychotherapeutic Considerations," *American Journal of Psychiatry*, vol. 140, no. 10, October 1983.

Kantrowitz, Barbara, and Wingert, Pat: "Step by Step," *Newsweek*, pp. 24–34.

Kiecolt-Glaser, Janice K.; Fisher, Laura D.; Ogrocki, Paula, et al: "Marital Quality, Marital Disruption, and Immune Function," *Psychosomatic Medicine*, vol. 49, no. 1, January/February 1987.

Latici, Elena: "Will He Love Your Kids? (and Will They Ever Accept Him?)," *New Woman*, May 1988, pp. 60–64.

Lauer, Robert H.: *Watersheds: Mastering Life's Unpredictable Crises*. Boston: Little, Brown, 1988.

Leahey, Maureen: "Findings From Research on Divorce: Implications for Professionals' Skill Development," *American Journal of Orthopsychiatry*, vol. 54, no. 2, April 1984.

Libman, Joan: "Step by Step," *Los Angeles Times*, January 5, 1990, pp. E-1,E-6,E-7.

Madara, Edward J., and Meese, Abigail: *The Self-Help Sourcebook, 2nd Edition*. Denville, N.J.: St. Clares-Riverside Medical Center, 1988.

————: *The Self-Help Sourcebook*. Denville, N.Y.: St. Clares-Riverside Medical Center, 1988.

McCann, Eileen, and Shannon, Douglas: *The Two-Step: The Dance Toward Intimacy*. New York: Grove Press, 1985.

McCranie, Edward W., and Kahan, Joel: "Personality and Multiple Divorce," *Journal of Nervous and Mental Disease*, vol. 174, no. 3, 1986.

Melichar, Joseph F., and Chiriboga, David A.: "Significance of Time in Adjustment to Marital Separation," *American Journal of Orthopsychiatry*, vol. 58, no. 2, April 1988.

Merikangas, Kathleen Ries: "Divorce and Assortative Mating Among Depressed Patients," *American Journal of Psychiatry*, vol. 141, no. 1, January 1984.

Rosen, Margery D.: "We Can't Stop Fighting," *Ladies' Home Journal*, February 1990, pp. 14, 16, 20.

Rounsaville, Bruce J.; Prusoff, Brigitte, and Weissman, Myrna: "The Course of Marital Disputes in Depressed Women: A 48-Month Follow-up Study," *Comprehensive Psychiatry*, vol. 21, no. 2, March/April 1980.

Ruestow, Paul; Dunner, David L., Bleecker, Bruce, and Fieve, Ronald R.: "Marital Adjustment in Primary Affective Disorder," *Comprehensive Psychiatry*, vol. 19, no. 6, November/December 1978.

Sack, Steven Mitchell: *The Complete Legal Guide to Marriage, Divorce, Custody, and Living Together*. New York: McGraw-Hill, 1987.

Samuelson, Elliot D.: *The Divorce Law Handbook*. New York: Human Sciences Press, 1988.

Sheehy, Gail: *Pathfinders*. New York: William Morrow, 1981.

Takas, Marianne: *Child Custody: A Complete Guide for Concerned Mothers*. New York: Harper & Row, 1987.

———: *Child Support*. New York: Harper & Row, 1985.

Wallerstein, Judith S.: *Helping the Family in Separation and Divorce: Advances in Theory and Practice*. New York: Basic Books, 1987.

Wilson, R. Reid: *Don't Panic: Taking Control of Anxiety Attacks*. New York: Harper & Row, 1986.

Witkin, Mildred Hope: *45—And Single Again*. New York: Dembner Books (Norton), 1985.

Woodruff, Robert A.; Guze, Samuel B., and Clayton, Paula J.: "Divorce Among Psychiatric Out-patients," *British Journal of Psychiatry,* vol. 121, 1972.

INDEX

A

Abuse
  divorce and, 21
  resources for, 140-141
Abusive marriages, 20
Acceptance, during recovery, 107
Addictions, recovery and, 104-105
Adjustment problems, 129
Age, attitudes toward, 72-73
Agoraphobia, 55-56
Alcohol abuse, 54-55
  resources for, 132-133
  signs of, 55
Aloneness, intimacy and, 75
Amends, making, 60-61
Anger, 7-8
  children and, 93
  denial of, 8
  during recovery, 106
  settlement and, 41-42
Antidepressant medication, 53
Anxiety disorders, 55-56
Assistance
  asking for, 5-6
  children and, 29-30
  discussing second thoughts with, 34
  fears concerning, 114-115
  reasons for, 110-111, 114
  when to get it, 52
Attorney
  leverage and, 41
  obtaining, 36-37
  settlement and, 45-46

B

Bargaining, during recovery, 106

C

Children
  actions to avoid, 84
  anger and, 93
  assistance with, 29-30
  conflict and, 79
  determining need for counseling,
    95-96
  discussing divorce with, 29-31, 79-82
  guidelines for, 30, 81-82
  divorce and, 130
  effects of divorce, 78-79
  age related, 88
  minimizing, 81, 86-88
  parents' communication and, 88-89

emotional tasks for, 92-94
  guilt and, 93
  health and, 13
  involving in divorce, 30
  lessons learned from divorce, 94
  loss and, 92-93
  providing emotional support for, 84-
    86
  reactions to divorce, 83
  remarriage and, 117-118
  second thoughts and, 33
  support groups for, 95
Closure, 107, 109
Codependent, 111
  definition of, 112
Communication, need for, 104
Confusion of divorce, 7
Coparenting, 89-92
  issues of, 90-91
  uncooperative partner, 92
Counseling
  sources of, 95, 133-134
  when to get it, 95-96

D

Dating, 72-76
  fears, 73-74
  as goal for recovery, 74-75
  safe dates, 74
Decision phase, 50-51
Denial, 7, 8, 25-27
  during recovery, 106
  price of, 27
Depression, 8
  during recovery, 107
  signs of, 53
Divorce
  characteristics of constructive, 108-
    109
  characterized, 24-25
  coping creatively, 48
  coping with, 4-5, 130
  guidelines for, 130-131
  legal, 5
  legal resources, 135-137
  readings, 137
  long term effects of, 100-101
  long term problems of, 99
  losses of, 3
  as opportunity for growth, 2
  phases of, 49-52

148